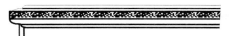
Anne M. Prouty Lynes
Editor

Lesbian Families' Challenges and Means of Resiliency: Implications for Feminist Family Therapy

Lesbian Families' Challenges and Means of Resiliency: Implications for Feminist Family Therapy has been co-published simultaneously as *Journal of Feminist Family Therapy*, Volume 18, Numbers 1/2 2006.

Pre-publication
REVIEWS,
COMMENTARIES,
EVALUATIONS . . .

More pre-publication
REVIEWS, COMMENTARIES, EVALUATIONS . . .

"AN OUTSTANDING ADDITION TO THE LITERATURE. . . . Covers a wide range of issues that are of central concern to mental health professionals working with lesbian women and their children, including the multiple stressors they encounter and the strength and resilience with which they address these stressors. . . . The literature reviews within the chapters provide EXCELLENT OVERVIEWS OF THE RELEVANT RESEARCH. . . . These reviews of the current research are not only useful for clinical work, but they also provide valuable information for challenging biased and misinformed social attitudes and oppressive social policies. . . . VERY EFFECTIVE IN COMMUNICATING THE COMPLEXITIES AND CHALLENGES OF LESBIAN EXPERIENCE. . . . Clinicians will greatly value the extent to which this book offers guidelines for their work with lesbian families."

Diane Kravetz, PhD
Professor, School of Social Work
University of Wisconsin-Madison
author of Tales from the Trenches:
Politics and Practice in Feminist
Service Organizations

"FULL OF IMPORTANT INSIGHTS about the challenges and resiliencies of these families from a multiplicity of therapeutic and research perspectives. . . . READABLE AND COHERENT, FILLED WITH ENGAGING, LUCID PROSE well laced with the *voices* of lesbians and their children who can provide therapists with an in-depth understanding of how to be aware of their own heterosexist biases and build respectful and facilitative relationships with lesbian families in practice. The explicit feminist lens threaded through all the chapters promotes a broad intersectional understanding of woman-loving relationships that crosses racial and ethnic and multiple other negotiated identities characterized by two women parenting their children together. Of particular value in this book is the attention in two of the chapters on the issue of violence among lesbian couples and the strategies that collaborative therapists can use to bring to light options for change."

Patricia O'Brien, PhD, MSW
Associate Professor
University of Illinois at Chicago

More pre-publication
REVIEWS, COMMENTARIES, EVALUATIONS . . .

"**A** MUST-HAVE RESOURCE FOR ANYONE WHO TEACHES A FAMILY THERAPY COURSE. Lyness pulls together top experts in the field of challenges faced by lesbian families who in turn offer AN EXCELLENT INTEGRATION OF THEORETICAL, EMPIRICAL, AND PRACTICAL PERSPECTIVES. The chapters offer compelling, novel, and meaningful reviews of the challenges faced by lesbian families. Beyond the classroom, this book serves as A TERRIFIC RESOURCE FOR PRACTITIONERS of family therapy and will better prepare family and individual therapists with awareness and knowledge of critical issues in relation to the treatment of all members in lesbian families. A validating reminder to therapists who believe in social justice and recognize the unhealthy aspects of living in a heterosexist world."

Nicholas Ladany, PhD
Chairperson
Department of Education
and Human Services
Lehigh University

"**T**he chapters of this book shine light on the needs and issues of sexual minorities both in maintaining relationsihips and in gaining support and acceptance from their families and society. As therapists, we cannot blissfully remain ignorant of these struggles. For anyone about to expand their practice or their thinking about gay and lesbian relationships, THIS BOOK WILL GIVE THEM MUCH NEEDED GUIDANCE."

Cleveland G. Shields, PhD
University of Rochester
School of Medicine

The Haworth Press, Inc.
New York

Lesbian Families' Challenges and Means of Resiliency: Implications for Feminist Family Therapy

Lesbian Families' Challenges and Means of Resiliency: Implications for Feminist Family Therapy has been co-published simultaneously as *Journal of Feminist Family Therapy*, Volume 18, Numbers 1/2 2006.

Monographic Separates from the *Journal of Feminist Family Therapy*®

For additional information on these and other Haworth Press titles, including descriptions, tables of contents, reviews, and prices, use the QuickSearch catalog at http://www.HaworthPress.com.

Lesbian Families' Challenges and Means of Resiliency: Implications for Feminist Family Therapy, edited by Anne M. Prouty Lyness, PhD, LMFT (Vol. 18, No. 1/2, 2006). *"Several really excellent chapters. . . . The resiliency materials are excellent and truly worth having." Laura S. Brown, PhD, ABPP, Independent Practice, Seattle, WA*

The Politics of the Personal in Feminist Family Therapy: International Examinations of Family Policy, edited by Anne M. Prouty Lyness, PhD, LMFT, (Vol. 17, No. 3/4, 2005). *Provides an interdisciplinary look at family public and social policies and the impact they have on families around the globe–all from a feminist perspective.*

Feminist Perspectives in Medical Family Therapy, edited by Anne M. Prouty Lyness, PhD, LMFT (Vol. 15, No. 2/3, 2003). *Explores the groundbreaking collaboration of therapy and medicine to form a biopsychosocial approach to health care, especially for women and families.*

Integrating Gender and Culture in Parenting, edited by Toni Schindler Zimmerman, PhD (Vol. 14, No. 3/4, 2002). *Presents specific strategies for parents to use to help children navigate gender terrain and resist stereotyping.*

Balancing Family and Work: Special Considerations in Feminist Therapy, edited by Toni Schindler Zimmerman, PhD (Vol. 13, No. 2/3, 2001). *"A must for many classrooms. . . . Relevant for family studies courses as well as clinical courses. This book covers a lot of ground. It's personal, political, conceptual, and clinical. It tells personal stories, discusses these people's struggles, and reports important research . . . An excellent introduction to the issues." (Volker Thomas, PhD, Associate Professor and Director, Marriage and Family Therapy Program, Purdue University, West Lafayette, IN)*

Integrating Gender and Culture in Family Therapy Training, edited by Toni Schindler Zimmerman, PhD (Vol. 12, No. 2/3 and 4, 2001). *"Engaging. . . . The predominant theme is infusion, not just inclusion. In a time when trainers, supervisors, trainees, supervisees, and clients are increasingly likely to come from diverse cultural backgrounds, this book will serve to keep us engaged in dialogue that addresses our own sexism, racism, and homophobia, and broadens our own cultural and gender lenses." (Janie Long, PhD, MFT Faculty, Purdue University, Indiana)*

Feminism, Community, and Communication, edited by Mary W. Olson, PhD, LICSW (Vol. 11, No. 4, 2000). *This important book rethinks therapy, research, teaching, and community work with a renewed emphasis on collaboration, intersubjectivity, and the process of communications as a world-making and identity-making activity. The issues of gender, culture, religion, race, and class figure prominently in this valuable book.*

Transformations of Gender and Race: Family and Developmental Perspectives, edited by Rhea V. Almeida, LCSW, DVS (Vol. 10, No. 1, 1998/99). *Offers superb contemporary thinking in cultural studies, post-colonial theory, gender theory, queer theory, and clinical and research work with numerous populations who have been overlooked and undertheorized.*

Reflections on Feminist Family Therapy Training, edited by Kathy Weingarten, PhD, and Michele Bograd, PhD (Vol. 8, No. 2, 1996). *"Those new to a feminist perspective on family therapy will find their eyes widened; experienced trainers will become immersed in the subjective dialogue." (Kathleen McGuire, PhD, Center for the Study of Women in Society, University of Oregon)*

Cultural Resistance: Challenging Beliefs About Men, Women, and Therapy, edited by Kathy Weingarten, PhD (Vol. 7, No. 1/2, 1995). *"It explores the possibilities for therapy to act in resistance to culturally constructed and dominant narratives that constrain therapists and our clients." (Australian New Zealand Journal of Family Therapy)*

Ethical Issues in Feminist Family Therapy, edited by Maryhelen Snyder, PhD (Vol. 6, No. 3, 1995). *"These deeply felt and tightly reasoned chapters . . . illuminate therapist positions that are more likely to foster just relations." (Kathy Weingarten, PhD, Co-Director, Program in Narrative Therapies, Family Institute of Cambridge, MA)*

Expansions of Feminist Family Theory Through Diversity, edited by Rhea V. Almeida, LCSW, DVS (Vol. 5, No. 3/4, 1994). *"Represents an important turning point in the history of family therapy. The authors explicitly address fundamental power differentials–based on race, gender, social class, and sexual orientation–that organize life for all families in America." (Robert-Jay Green, PhD, Professor and Coordinator of Family/Child Psychology Training, California School of Professional Psychology, Berkeley)*

Feminism and Addiction, edited by Claudia Bepko, MSW (Vol. 3, No. 3/4, 1992). *"Provides valuable clinical information for therapists working with alcohol- and drug-addicted women. It describes methods of therapeutic training and intervention based on an integration of feminist theory and other major theories that expand the boundaries of treatment for addicted women." (Contemporary Psychology)*

Feminist Approaches for Men in Family Therapy, edited by Michele Bograd, PhD (Vol. 2, No. 3/4, 1991). *"A new offering that marriage and family therapists will find to be a valuable addition and resource." (Journal of Family Psychotherapy)*

Lesbian Families' Challenges and Means of Resiliency: Implications for Feminist Family Therapy

Anne M. Prouty Lyness
Editor

Lesbian Families' Challenges and Means of Resiliency: Implications for Feminist Family Therapy has been co-published simultaneously as *Journal of Feminist Family Therapy*, Volume 18, Numbers 1/2 2006.

The Haworth Press, Inc.

New York • London • Victoria (AU)
www.HaworthPress.com

Lesbian Families' Challenges and Means of Resiliency: Implications for Feminist Family Therapy has been co-published simultaneously as *Journal of Feminist Family Therapy®*, Volume 18, Numbers 1/2 2006.

The development, preparation, and publication of this work has been undertaken with great care. However, the publisher, employees, editors, and agents of The Haworth Press and all imprints of The Haworth Press, Inc., including The Haworth Medical Press® and Pharmaceutical Products Press®, are not responsible for any errors contained herein or for consequences that may ensue from use of materials or information contained in this work. With regard to case studies, identities and circumstances of individuals discussed herein have been changed to protect confidentiality. Any resemblance to actual persons, living or dead, is entirely coincidental.

The Haworth Press is committed to the dissemination of ideas and information according to the highest standards of intellectual freedom and the free exchange of ideas. Statements made and opinions expressed in this publication do not necessarily reflect the views of the Publisher, Directors, management, or staff of The Haworth Press, Inc., or an endorsement by them.

Cover design by Marylouise E. Doyle

Library of Congress Cataloging-in-Publication Data

Lesbian families' challenges and means of resiliency : implications for feminist family therapy / Anne M. Prouty Lyness, editor.
     p. cm.
"Co-published simultaneously as Journal of feminist family therapy, volume 18, numbers 1/2 2006."
    Includes bibliographical references and index.
    ISBN-13: 978-0-7890-3427-4 (hard cover : alk. paper)
    ISBN-10: 0-7890-3427-1 (hard cover : alk. paper)
    ISBN-13: 978-0-7890-3428-1 (soft cover : alk. paper)
    ISBN-10: 0-7890-3428-X (soft cover : alk. paper)
    1. Lesbian mothers. 2. Lesbian couples. 3. Lesbians–Family relationships. 4. Lesbians–Counseling of. 5. Family psychotherapy. 6. Feminist therapy. 7. Resilience (Personality trait) I. Prouty Lyness, Anne M. II. Journal of feminist family therapy.
  HQ75.53.L47 2006
  306.874'308664–dc22
                                     2006015688

Indexing, Abstracting & Website/Internet Coverage

This section provides you with a list of major indexing & abstracting services and other tools for bibliographic access. That is to say, each service began covering this periodical during the year noted in the right column. Most Websites which are listed below have indicated that they will either post, disseminate, compile, archive, cite or alert their own Website users with research-based content from this work. (This list is as current as the copyright date of this publication.)

Abstracting, Website/Indexing Coverage . . . . Year When Coverage Began

- *Alternative Press Index (print, online & CD-ROM from NISC).*
  The most complete guide to alternative & radical media.
  <http://www.altpress.org> **2005**

- *Applied Social Sciences Index & Abstracts (ASSIA)*
  (Cambridge Scientific Abstracts) (Online: ASSI via Data-Star)
  (CD-ROM: ASSIA Plus) <http://www.csa.com> **1996**

- *Contemporary Women's Issues* **1998**

- *Criminal Justice Abstracts* **2001**

- *EBSCOhost Electronic Journals Service (EJS)*
  <http://ejournals.ebsco.com> **2001**

- *Elsevier Scopus <http://www.info.scopus.com>* **2005**

- *e-psyche, LLC <http://www.e-psyche.net>* **2001**

- *Family Index Database <http://www.familyscholar.com>* **1995**

- *Family & Society Studies Worldwide <http://www.nisc.com>* **1996**

- *Family Violence & Sexual Assault Bulletin* **1992**

- *Feminist Periodicals: A Current Listing of Contents* **1992**

- *GenderWatch <http://www.slinfo.com>* **1998**

- *Google <http://www.google.com>* **2004**

- *Google Scholar <http://scholar.google.com>* **2004**

(continued)

(continued)

Special Bibliographic Notes related to special journal issues (separates) and indexing/abstracting:

- indexing/abstracting services in this list will also cover material in any "separate" that is co-published simultaneously with Haworth's special thematic journal issue or DocuSerial. Indexing/abstracting usually covers material at the article/chapter level.
- monographic co-editions are intended for either non-subscribers or libraries which intend to purchase a second copy for their circulating collections.
- monographic co-editions are reported to all jobbers/wholesalers/approval plans. The source journal is listed as the "series" to assist the prevention of duplicate purchasing in the same manner utilized for books-in-series.
- to facilitate user/access services all indexing/abstracting services are encouraged to utilize the co-indexing entry note indicated at the bottom of the first page of each article/chapter/contribution.
- this is intended to assist a library user of any reference tool (whether print, electronic, online, or CD-ROM) to locate the monographic version if the library has purchased this version but not a subscription to the source journal.
- individual articles/chapters in any Haworth publication are also available through the Haworth Document Delivery Service (HDDS).

Lesbian Families' Challenges and Means of Resiliency: Implications of Feminist Family Therapy

CONTENTS

ABOUT THE EDITOR

Anne M. Prouty Lyness, PhD, LMFT, is Associate Professor and Director of Clinical Training in the Marriage and Family Therapy program within the Department of Applied Psychology at Antioch University-New England in Keene, New Hampshire. Anne earned her masters degree in Marriage and Family Therapy from East Carolina University and her doctorate from Purdue University. She has a lifelong interest in feminism and her writing reflects her clinical and research interests in women's health and the importance of focusing on human diversity and marginalized voices in therapy, training, and research. This is her fourth year as Editor of the *Journal of Feminist Family Therapy*, and she is honored to be able to work with such distinguished and dedicated feminists such as the authors in this very special volume.

About the Contributors

Colleen M. Connolly, PhD, is Associate Professor in the Professional Counseling Program at Texas State University-San Marcos. She is a counselor educator in marriage and family emphasis and also a Licensed Professional Counselor. Her primary qualitative research interests involve lesbian women and couples. Colleen served as President of the Association of Gay, Lesbian, and Bisexual Issues in Counseling (AGLBIC), a division of the American Counseling Association (2003-2004). She also co-founded the AGLBIC of Texas, a division of the Texas Counseling Association, and served as the Charter President (2000-2002).

Judith C. Daniluk, PhD, is Professor in the Department of Educational and Counseling Psychology at the University of British Columbia. Her primary clinical and research expertise is in the area of women's sexuality and reproductive health. She is particularly interested in the psychosocial consequences of infertility and collaborative, third-party reproduction.

Lisa Giddings, PhD, is Associate Professor of Economics at the University of Wisconsin-La Crosse. Her research interests include the effects of transition in Central and Eastern Europe on the economic circumstances of women and minorities. She has published articles in *Feminist Economics, the Eastern Economics Journal* and the *Economics of Transition.* She has only recently begun to write creative non-fiction and fiction, most likely in response to becoming a parent. In addition to the girl in the story published here, she and her partner are celebrating the recent birth of a baby boy.

A. Cassandra Golding is a Clinical Psychology PhD student at the University of Rhode Island who studies LGBT issues and has conducted several research projects concerning therapy with LGBT clients, lesbian couples, LGBT families, origins of homosexuality, childhood trauma, autonomy, and the power of emotion. She is also a clinical interventionist for projects Reduce and Dial at Rhode Island hospital as well as the group facilitator for the RYDD (Reduce Youth Dangerous Driving) program for which she's writing a manualized treatment. She has presented workshops for URI and Brown University on the unique relationship patterns of lesbian couples as they relate to all women. She currently works with Lisa Bowleg, PhD. Cassandra has been the clinical psychology student representative and inter-department liaison as well as a member of the Multicultural Task Force. In addition to these facilitations, Cassandra is also a student affiliate of Psi Chi and the APA.

Karen C. Kranz, PhD, is a graduate from the Department of Educational and Counseling Psychology at the University of British Columbia. Her research interests include mother-daughter relationships, lesbians' experiences of self-disclosing their lesbianism, and lesbian-led families. She is a therapist in private practice in Vancouver, Canada working with women and men: individuals, couples, and families.

Deanna Linville, PhD, LMFT, is Assistant Professor in the Marriage and Family Therapy Program in the School of Education at the University of Oregon. She also serves as the clinical director for the Center for Family Therapy and the lead therapist for RainRock, a new eating disorder residential treatment program. Her research publications include topics such as: Domestic Violence, Eating Disorders, Collaborative Family Healthcare, and International Adoption. Additionally, she has been an active member of QREAD (Queer research, education, advocacy, and dialogue) since its inception in the summer of 2004, which serves to promote, support, and recognize all facets of LGBTQ people's identities. In 2005, she was awarded the Commitment to LGBT Community Award.

Charles Negy, PhD, obtained his doctorate in Clinical Psychology from Texas A&M University in 1994. Currently, he is Associate Professor and Director of Clinical Training at the University of Central Florida. As a licensed psychologist, he limits the psychological services he provides to Spanish-speaking Hispanic families and children. His research interests vary and focus primarily on population variables such as ethnicity, acculturation, gender, social class, and sexual orientation. Specifically, Dr. Negy is interested in knowing how these variables influence people's attitudes and behaviors, including performance on personality tests.

Cliff McKinney, MS, completed his BA in Psychology at the Florida Institute of Technology and currently is in his fourth year in the Clinical Psychology PhD program at the University of Central Florida. His interests in clinical psychology are focused primarily on parent-child interactions, factors that are associated with adaptive and maladaptive outcomes for children and adolescents, and childhood disruptive behavior disorders.

Suzanne R. Merlis, PsyD, is a licensed Clinical Psychologist and Director of Mental Health Services for The Center for Torture and Trauma in Decatur, Georgia. Over the past ten years, she has specialized in providing services to individuals who have survived severe traumatic experiences including rape, domestic violence, sexual abuse, torture, and acute and chronic illness. She did her post-doctoral training in Family Systems and Health and continues to work collaboratively with healthcare providers to enhance their understanding, integration, and treatment of the effects of trauma on physical and psychological health. Her clinical and research interests reflect a path informed by feminist thought and dedication to the diverse voices of those who have been disempowered through oppression and violence. She also serves on a number of boards and community organizations committed to improving the lives of marginalized groups. Additionally, Dr. Merlis works with individuals, couples, and families in her private practice in Atlanta, Georgia.

Cynthia Ring, BS, is a second-year student in the MSW Program at The Ohio State University, Columbus. She has worked for a social services agency that helps women recently released from state correctional facilities adjust to living in the community.

Dr. Bette Speziale, PhD, is Associate Professor in the College of Social Work at The Ohio State University, Columbus. She teaches courses in the Master's and Doctoral Programs including individual, couple, and family systems functioning, women's issues, crisis intervention, and qualitative research methods. Her qualitative research interests are couples' and women's lived experiences and multiple realities.

Editor's Foreword

I am excited to coordinate this volume of work that focuses on lesbian couples and the families they create together. I wanted to gather feminist family clinicians and clinician-researchers together to examine a few of the current difficulties these women are facing in constructing family–but to do so in a balanced way through the lens of resiliency. In this way we, as family therapists, honor the process of the family. We treat relationships as journeys instead of arbitrarily punctuated circumstances. In thinking about relationships as journeys, this allows us to notice the social constructions of oppression, to work together as communities of feminists to create social change, and to celebrate the ever-changing nature of our relationships with each other and the larger cultures. Knowing our lives and our work are journeys empowers us to remain resilient.

But resiliency is not about "feel good feminism" (Hare-Mustin, 1986). Froma Walsh (1998) talks about resiliency as being able to struggle well and I have found this to be a very empowering construction of resiliency: It is relational and process-focused. Lesbian couples choose how to construct their couplehood, their parenting, their family membership, and their unfolding family stories; and do so within the larger context of multiple oppressions like heterosexism, sexism, and racism. Lesbian women's stories are complex stories of struggles and triumphs along the journey of being a family: of struggling well.

This volume honors lesbian-led families by giving voice to their experiences. Karen Kranz's and Judith Daniluk's study provides a look at lesbian couples' complex decision-making processes and experiences becoming parents via anonymous donor insemination. Looking a little further along the developmental lifespan, Cassandra Golding shares the

[Haworth co-indexing entry note]: "Editor's Foreword." Lyness, Anne M. Prouty. Co-published simultaneously in *Journal of Feminist Family Therapy* (The Haworth Press, Inc.) Vol. 18, No. 1/2, 2006, pp. xxiii-xxiv; and: *Lesbian Families' Challenges and Means of Resiliency: Implications for Feminist Family Therapy* (ed: Anne M. Prouty Lyness) The Haworth Press, Inc., 2006, pp.xix-xx. Single or multiple copies of this article are available for a fee from The Haworth Document Delivery Service [1-800-HAWORTH, 9:00 a.m. - 5:00 p.m. (EST). E-mail address: docdelivery@haworthpress.com].

xix

results of her interviews of lesbian parents' experiences of creating families and rearing their children. This is followed by a poignant personal reflection by Lisa Giddings about her kindergarten-age daughter's encounter with heterosexism about lesbian marriage. Charles Negy and Cliff McKinney then provide a description of how they have applied several key feminist therapy ideas to affirm and empower lesbian couples as they help their children to deal with heterosexism in therapy.

The next two works focus on the issue of violence in intimate relationships. Bette Speziale and Cynthia Ring review the literature, examining aspects of violence in lesbian relationships and community responses. Suzanne R. Merlis and Deanna Linville provide the thick description of several Chicago area clinicians' experiences of a lesbian community's diverse and complex responses to domestic violence. In her study, Colleen Connolly then refocuses our attention to lesbian couples' resiliency processes in the face of multiple stressors. She provides an in-depth review of the feminist family therapy and counseling literatures while humanizing the themes with quotes from women from her research.

This volume provides a glimpse into several aspects of lesbian women's lives in couples, families, and as communities of women. I hope that professionals working with lesbian women and their families continue to use feminist-informed methods to help us all learn more about lesbian women's needs and experiences throughout the lifespan and how we are empowering lesbian-led families in therapy. I hope that future submissions to *Journal of Feminist Family Therapy* provide a richer description of ethnic, religious, age, and ability diversities so that our understanding of how lesbian couples and families struggle well continues to deepen and enrich our practices, our research, and our lives. We need to know more about lesbian couples' and lesbian-led families' journeys and their methods of struggling well across the lifespan. For the continued resiliency of feminism, it is essential that lesbian couples' complex and diverse journeys are better known, meaningfully supported, and openly celebrated.

Anne M. Prouty Lyness, PhD, LMFT

REFERENCES

Hare-Mustin, R. (1986). The problem of gender in family therapy theory. *Family Process, 26,* 15-27.
Walsh, F. (1998). *Strengthening family resilience.* New York: Guilford.

Living Outside of the Box:
Lesbian Couples with Children
Conceived Through the Use
of Anonymous Donor Insemination

Karen C. Kranz
Judith C. Daniluk

SUMMARY. There is a dearth of research that exclusively explores the lives and experiences of lesbian couples who conceived their children through the use of anonymous donor insemination–an option that has only recently become more widely available to lesbians. The question that guided this qualitative inquiry was: "How do lesbian couples with children conceived through the use of anonymous donor insemination live as, and experience, family?" Interviews were conducted with 10 couples who self-identified as lesbian, chose to have their children while in their lesbian relationships, and conceived their children through the use of anonymous donor insemination. An interpretive interactionist analysis of the transcripts revealed that the following four thematic areas

Address correspondence to: Judith C. Daniluk, PhD, Department of Educational and Counseling Psychology, University of British Columbia, 2125 Main Mall, Vancouver, British Columbia, Canada V6T 1Z3 (E-mail: judith.daniluk@ubc.com).

The authors wish to thank all of the participants for sharing their experiences for the purpose of this research. The first author was supported by funding from the Social Sciences and Humanities Research Council of Canada, the Killam Trusts, and the UBC Faculty of Education Research Office of Graduate Programs and Research.

[Haworth co-indexing entry note]: "Living Outside of the Box: Lesbian Couples with Children Conceived Through the Use of Anonymous Donor Insemination." Kranz, Karen C., and Judith C. Daniluk. Co-published simultaneously in *Journal of Feminist Family Therapy* (The Haworth Press, Inc.) Vol. 18, No. 1/2, 2006, pp. 1-33; and: *Lesbian Families' Challenges and Means of Resiliency: Implications for Feminist Family Therapy* (ed: Anne M. Prouty Lyness) The Haworth Press, Inc., 2006, pp. 1-33. Single or multiple copies of this article are available for a fee from The Haworth Document Delivery Service [1-800-HAWORTH, 9:00 a.m. - 5:00 p.m. (EST). E-mail address: docdelivery@haworthpress.com].

1

shaped, constructed, represented, and gave meaning to these unique family configurations: conception options of two women; two women parenting; anonymous donors/not fathers; and families with lesbian mothers. These are discussed in terms of their implications for therapists working with lesbian-led families. doi:10.1300/J086v18n01_01 *[Article copies available for a fee from The Haworth Document Delivery Service: 1-800-HAWORTH. E-mail address: <docdelivery@haworthpress.com> Website: <http://www.HaworthPress.com> © 2006 by The Haworth Press, Inc. All rights reserved.]*

KEYWORDS. Lesbian family, couple therapy, lesbian couple therapy, feminist couple and family therapy, feminist research, parenting, donor insemination, qualitative research

INTRODUCTION

On 11 October 1987 over 200,000 people from around the United States marched on Washington, D.C., for lesbian and gay rights. One button worn by many lesbians read "Love is What Makes a Family." (Riley, 1988)

The landscape of the traditional two-parent family is shifting to include a "wide variety of alternative family forms including the lesbian-parented household" (O'Connell, 1992, p. 281). The growing number of lesbian (and gay) parents represents a "sociocultural innovation that is unique to the current historical era" (Patterson, 1995a, p. 263). In fact, referring to the burgeoning number of lesbians choosing to parent since the early 1980s, Arnup (1998) coined the term "lesbian baby-boom." This increasing trend for lesbian women to embrace motherhood was underscored by Tulchinsky (1999):

> . . . in the '70s lesbians were too busy organizing music festivals, leading Gay Pride Parades, counseling at women's shelters, playing softball, operating coffee houses and fighting for equal rights. But in the early to mid '80s, many women realized that "lesbian mothers" was not an oxymoron, and the lesbian baby boom began. Gay women all over North America traded their picket signs for picket fences, motorcycles for strollers, flannel shirts for nursing bras, and leather jackets for leather teething rings. (p. E5)

Several forces are associated with the increase in the number of lesbians choosing to parent. The 1973 decision by the American Psychiatric Association to remove homosexuality from its list of mental disorders (Kirpatrick, 1990; Stein, 1988) has served to help legitimize homosexual relationships. Gay political activism for social and legal rights has increased the visibility, and to a degree, acceptance of homosexuality (Stein, 1988). The reorganization of gender-roles and gender relations within families resulting from the feminist movement has made visible and helped legitimize a wider range of family forms (Alldred, 1998; Lempert & DeVault, 2000; Thorne, 1992). The extension of educational and employment opportunities for women also has "enabled increasing numbers of Western women to construct independent identities and lifestyles beyond traditional marriage, motherhood, and indeed, heterosexuality" (Dunne, 2000, p. 11). Increased access to the use of anonymous donor sperm has given lesbian couples the opportunity to create their own unique families outside the traditional heterosexual context and without the active involvement of male partners (Dunne, 2000; Haimes & Weiner, 2000; Riley, 1988). Perhaps most important are the changes in social and legal policies which have made lesbian families more acceptable in the eyes of the law, and parenting a more viable option for lesbians.

The majority of lesbians, particularly prior to 1980, became mothers through former heterosexual relationships (Arnup, 1997; Kaufman & Dundas, 1995; Patterson, 1996). As such, most of the research in the 1970s and 1980s focused on lesbian mothers who came out as lesbians after having conceived their children in heterosexual relationships (Alexander, 1997). Much of this research examined the psychological adjustment and parenting skills of lesbian mothers versus heterosexual mothers and compared the social, psychological, and sexual development of children raised by lesbian moms to that of children raised by heterosexual moms (Gartrell et al., 1996). Heterosexist assumptions underlying this research placed heterosexual mothers and mothering as the standard against which lesbian mothers were compared and assessed.

Ironically, the findings of many of these studies (e.g., Kweskin & Cook, 1982; Miller, Jacobson, & Bigner, 1982; Mucklow & Phelan, 1979) support the mental health, maternal attitudes, and psychological adjustment of lesbian women. Lesbian parents do not appear to differ from heterosexual parents in terms of their competence as parents (e.g., Bos, van Balen, & van den Boom, 2004). Likewise, there is evidence that children raised by lesbians are no more likely than children raised by heterosexual mothers to experience social, psychological, cognitive, and/or sexual development difficulties (Golombok, Spencer, & Rutter, 1983; Golombok et al., 2003; Golombok & Tasker, 1996; Green, Mandel, Hotvedt, Gray, & Smith, 1986; Hoeffer, 1981; Huggins, 1989; Javaid, 1993; Kirpatrick, Smith, & Roy, 1981; Tasker & Golombok, 1995). The main conclusion drawn from the above studies is that lesbian mothers and their children are very similar to, rather than different from, hetero-sexual mothers and their children.

At first glance, this conclusion appears positive. According to Stacey and Biblarz (2001) it has "promoted a gradual liberalizing trend in judi-cial and policy decisions" related to child custody and adoption peti-tions by lesbians. However, as Pollack (1992) aptly notes, this line of inquiry makes "us [lesbians] more invisible, and it obscures the radical alternative lesbian lives can model" (p. 219). Additionally, this perspec-tive also holds heterosexual motherhood as the standard against which all other mothers are compared. Thus, "a lesbian mother must portray herself as being as close to the All-American norm as possible–the spit-ting image of her heterosexual counterpart–and preferably asexual" (Polikoff, 1992, p. 229). Finally, studies that seek to discover the degree to which lesbian mothers and their children are comparable to hetero-sexual mothers and their children speak to the heteronormative assump-tions about family that abound in North American culture, and serve to reinforce the "social and institutional support that privileges heterosex-ual families" (Clarke, 2002, p. 212).

Today there are more options available for lesbians who wish to have children, on their own or with a partner. Lesbians can self-inseminate with sperm donated by a friend or family member, adopt (most often in-ternationally), or engage in heterosexual intercourse exclusively for the purpose of procreation. They can also turn to fertility clinics and be in-seminated with the sperm of an anonymous donor provided by one of the many sperm banks in North America (Boyd, 1998; Falk, 1994; Hare, 1994; Pies, 1988; Shore, 1996)–a family building service that has only recently become more widely available to lesbians (Englert, 1994; Haimes & Weiner, 2000). For many decades lesbian families were deemed threatening to the dominant notion of what constitutes a legiti-mate family (Haimes & Weiner, 2000). As Evans (1990) states, lesbian women choosing to conceive through the use of anonymous donor in-semination "implies a kind of self-sufficiency which is threatening to the patriarchal order of society" (p. 45), in that this challenges the perva-sive societal belief that it is every child's right to have a mother and a fa-ther (Englert, 1994). It has only been in the last 10 to 15 years that fertility clinics have started to relax the restrictions on lesbians' access to services, as lesbian-led families become more common and legally sanctioned (Nelson, 1996; Pies; 1987).

It should not be surprising, then, that we know very little about the needs and experiences of lesbian women who elect to create their families through the use of anonymous donor insemination. A few studies have been conducted that compared lesbian and heterosexual families, both with children conceived with donor sperm (e.g., Chan, Brooks, Raboy, & Patterson, 1998; Golombok, 1999; Jacob, Klock, & Maier, 1999; Vanfraussen, Ponjaert-Kristoffersen, & Brewaeys, 2003). The research focused on lesbian-led families with children include children brought into these families through adoption or former heterosexual relationships, as well as those conceived through known and anonymous donor sperm (e.g., Dunne, 2000; Gartrell et al., 1996; Gartrell et al., 1999; Gartrell et al., 2000; Patterson, 1997, 1995a, 1995b, 1994, Patterson, Hurt, & Mason, 1998; Stevens, Perry, Burston, Golombok, & Golding, 2003).

Only two published studies, Wilson (2000) and Brewaeys, Devroey, Helmerhorst, Van Hall, and Ponjaert (1995), exclusively focused on examining family life for lesbian couples whose children were conceived through the use of anonymous donor insemination. In her grounded-theory study Wilson explored the parenting roles of lesbian co-mothers by conducting open-ended, telephone interviews with nine co-mothers whose partners conceived their children through donor insemination. The non-gestational co-mothers in this study, felt legitimate as mothers when they received legal recognition; recognized that their children will likely experience discrimination as children of lesbians and were committed to being out and open with their children and in their lives; created equal parenting relationships based on shared values with their partners; found that making the decision of which woman in the couple would be the birth mother was relatively easy; and felt that extended family acceptance of their mothering roles helped build their confidence as mothers.

Brewaeys et al. (1995) asked lesbian couples who entered the anonymous donor insemination programme at the Centre of Reproductive Medicine at the University Hospital in Brussels, Belgium between 1986 and 1991, to take part in a longitudinal study of the disclosure and anonymity attitudes, and parenting roles of lesbian-led families. Survey data were collected on 50 lesbian couples at the start of the inseminations and between the children's first and second years using a questionnaire developed by the researchers. Subsequent to the birth of their babies, 56% ($n = 100$) of these mothers said they wished the donors

were registered with a central registry containing non-identifying information that could be made available to their children when they reach
adulthood, while only 10% would have chosen to do so at the time of insemination. The reason given for this shift was that at the time of insemination these mothers wanted to avoid interference from third parties.
However, at the time of the second interview they said they were more
focused on the needs of their children. These mothers felt their children
might want information regarding their social and medical histories. Of
note, for 12 of the 50 couples, birth mothers were in favor of donor identity registration, while the non-gestational mothers were not, suggesting
perhaps that donor identity was perceived as more threatening to the
mothers who did not have the benefit of having a genetic tie to their children. All of the participants in this study planned to tell their children
how they were conceived; all wanted to be clear with their children that
donors were not fathers; and when given the opportunity, each couple
made a point of using the same donor when they had their second child.
In terms of negotiating parenting roles, most couples shared parenting
and employment and planned to tell their children about their lesbianism.

Following from these two studies, the purpose of this study was to
further enhance our understanding of the ways in which lesbian couples
whose children are conceived through the use of anonymous donor insemination–without the possibility or threat of "paternal" entitlement or
involvement–shape, construct, represent and give meaning to their families. The research question guiding this inquiry was: *How do lesbian
couples, with children conceived through the use of anonymous donor
insemination, live as, and experience, family?*

METHOD

The qualitative method that guided this research was interpretive
interactionism (Denzin, 1989a, 2001). The interpretive interactionist researcher examines "slices, sequences, and instances of social interaction" (Denzin, 1989, p. 26). Subjective personal experiences are interpreted in order to understand the meanings, intentions, and actions of
participants. By studying biographical experiences that occur in social
interactions, interpretive interactionism strives to connect personal experiences to the "larger historical, institutional, and cultural arenas" that
surround a person's life (Denzin, 1989, p. 17). Such a position is critical
if we are to begin to understand the lives and experiences of lesbians

whose families challenge long-held beliefs and values about the centrality of fathers and the privileging of genetic ties in the lives of children and in the social construction of family. Interpretive interactionism "fits itself to the relation between the individual and society, to the nexus of biography and society" (p. 139) and attempts to understand how a sequence of social interactions or social experiences are organized, perceived, and constructed by interacting individuals (Denzin, 1989)–in this case the social interactions and experiences related to how the participant couples lived and experienced their families.

Participants

Ten lesbian couples who together conceived their children and created their families through the use of anonymous donor insemination participated in this research. Participants were recruited through word-of-mouth and advertisements posted in a number of locations that lesbian mothers were likely to frequent, and in local publications and list-serves that were likely to be read by lesbians. Additionally, participants were recruited through a private west-coast fertility centre. Couples were asked to telephone or e-mail the researchers if they were interested in participating in this research. We had hoped to interview couples who were diverse in terms of socioeconomic, educational, racial, and ethnic group memberships. However, a relatively homogeneous group of participants volunteered for the study (i.e., primarily Caucasian women of Western European descent, highly educated, affluent).

Group demographic profile–First interview. At the time of the first interview, the 20 women in this study ranged in age from 31 to 42 years and had been in their relationships for between 6 and 19 years. They had a total of 16 children conceived through the use of donor insemination. The children ranged in age from 1 1/2 years to 6 years. Five couples had one child, four couples had two children and one couple had three children. Nineteen of the women were of Western European descent and one woman was of Asian descent. All but one of the donors selected by these women was Caucasian. One family chose an Asian donor. In three of the couples, both women were employed full-time. In five couples, one mother worked part-time and the other mother worked full-time. In one family, both mothers worked part-time and in another family, one mother parented full-time and the other mother was employed full-time. In seven couples, one mother was the birth mother. In the other three couples, both mothers wanted to be birth mothers. In the three families in which both mothers wanted to be birth mothers, at the time of the first interview, two mothers were pregnant and the third was in the insemination process. The women in this study were highly educated (i.e., five had professional degrees or Doctorates, five had Master's degrees, four had Bachelor degrees, two had College certificates, and the education level of four women was unknown). In terms of employment these women held a variety of professional occupations in fields including business administration and finance, health care, law enforcement, education, and creative arts.

Group demographic profile–Validation interview. In the 24-30 months between the data collection and validation interviews an additional five children were born to these 10 couples. In two families, the mother who was biologically related to their first child gave birth to their second child. In two families, the other partner gave birth to the couples' second child. In the other family, due to fertility challenges faced by the second mother, the first mother gestated the genetic child of her partner following IVF. Seven of the original 10 couples participated in the validation interviews. In four of these families, the split between parenting and employment remained similar to the division at the time of the first interview. In the other three families one mother shifted from part-time employment to full-time parenting, another mother shifted from full-time employment to two-thirds time employment, and in the third family, one mother reduced her employment from full-time to part-time.

Procedure

Interviews were conducted with couples in their homes. The first author, a childless doctoral student in a long-term lesbian relationship, conducted the in-depth, audiotaped interviews. The intent was to capture the meanings and experiences of family for these lesbian couples. Given our interactionist assumption that such meanings are created through interactions between the mothers, the mothers were interviewed as a couple. The interviews were semi-structured and comprised of open-ended questions. Because the material addressed in the present study was of a personal nature, it was important at the outset for the participants to feel safe and comfortable. "Empathic rapport" (Osborne, 1990) was established through engaging in casual conversation. When the couple and the first author became comfortable with each other, issues of confidentiality were addressed. Couples were assured that we were not interested in making moral judgments about their experiences, but rather were interested in understanding their experiences. Participants were asked to read and sign two copies of an ethical consent and were reminded that their involvement was voluntary and that they were free to withdraw from the study at any time. After the participants had an opportunity to ask questions, the interviewer read a statement reiterating the purpose of the study and orienting them to the interview, asking them to tell their story of creating and living as a family as lesbian mothers with a child (or children) conceived through the use of anonymous donor insemination.

The interviewer assisted the couples in describing their experiences and in making interpretations of these experiences. The interviews were semi-structured and comprised of open-ended questions. We had a general list of questions that we sought to have answered (e.g., What does a typical day look like). The phrasing of the questions and the order in which they were asked were modified to fit with each participant couple's narrative. To help the participants in the narration of their stories, the interviewer used advanced empathy, paraphrasing, and reflection, and attended to the participants' verbal and non-verbal responses. Clarifying and open-ended probing questions that deepened the mothers' exploration of significant issues that were raised during the interviews were asked (e.g., "You mentioned____could you say more about that?" "How did you feel about ____?"). Interviews lasted approximately 90 minutes.

Analysis of the Interactional Texts

The outcome of this interpretive interactionist research was a thick interpretation that is presented as follows as conceptual categories, or themes. These themes describe how "social experience, or a sequence of social interactions is organized, perceived, and constructed by interacting individuals" (Denzin, 1989a, p. 24)–in this case how the couples in this study organized, perceived and constructed family. There were three phases in the analysis of the interactional texts: bracketing, construction, and contextualization. "Bracketing" involved dissecting the interactional texts in order to uncover, define, and analyze the elements and essential structures of the lived experience of family for the participants in the study. In this phase of the research process the tapes were transcribed and resulted in approximately 700 pages of single-spaced text. The text was then subdivided into key experiential units (i.e., key phrases and statements that pertained directly to the topic being explored). The meanings of the experiential units were identified and examined to reveal the essential, recurring features of family, as experienced and described by the participants.

In the construction phase of the interpretive interactionism research
. process, an attempt was made to "re-create lived experience in terms of its constituent, analytic elements" (Denzin, 1989a, p. 59). More specifically, the meanings of the experiential units were connected to other units within the story. To do this all of the meanings of the experiential units were listed and ordered as they occurred within the process. At this point, the experiential units were organized into conceptual categories, that is, the four thematic areas, identified and discussed below.

In the third phase of the research process, contextualization, the goal was to locate the topic under study in the personal biographies and the social environments of the women being studied (Denzin, 1989a, 2001). This phase involved describing, in full detail, the essential features of the experiences of family as identified in the previous stages of bracketing and construction. The main themes of the stories were compared and synthesized so that their differences could be brought together in a reformulated statement of the experiences and meanings of family for the lesbian couples in this study, all of whom had created their families through the use of anonymous donor insemination.

The final product of this research was written in a form Denzin (1989a, 2001) refers to as an interpretive-narrative. The interpretive-narrative was written so that the interpretations of the participants were merged with our interpretations. To do this, quotes from the participants' narratives were included to elucidate our interpretations. Thus, the final product was multi-voiced and dialogical.

Validation Interviews

As interpretations that are developed about a participant's life must be understood by the participant, a copy of the findings with an explanatory letter was mailed to each of the participant couples. Three couples were not available for a validation interview–one due to the dissolution of their relationship. Interviews were set up with the other seven couples. During the tape-recorded validation interviews, changes in participants' family structures (e.g., additional children) were noted, as were other relevant changes in their roles and family lives (e.g., shifts in employment, children entering school). Each couple was asked whether the descriptions and interpretations extracted from the data resonated with their experiences. All couples confirmed that their own experiences were indeed represented in the findings. Many also noted with interest, the variations in experiences between couples that were reflected within the four themes. The validation interviews lasted between 60 and 90 minutes.

FINDINGS

In these lesbian-led families with children conceived through the use of anonymous donor insemination, the children were parented by their biological mothers and their non-biological mothers. Their gestational, relational and genetic family backgrounds included a biological mother, a non-biological mother, and an anonymous donor. The interviews with the 10 lesbian couples in this study revealed four interrelated themes that reflected how these women shaped, constructed, represented, and gave meaning to their families. These themes were:

- Conception Options of Two Women
- Two Women Parenting
- Anonymous Donors/Not Fathers
- Families with Lesbian Mothers

Each of these themes is comprised of interactions between the mothers, between the mothers and their children, between the families and their extended family members, and between the families and society. The four themes described a process that began with the first theme (i.e., conception options of two women). The three remaining themes described the ongoing process of living family life as lesbian couples with children conceived through the use of anonymous donor insemination. These three themes will continue to evolve in the participants' lives–shifting and changing as the children experience each development phase, as social and legal policies concerning homosexuality and reproductive technology progress or regress, and as the families continue to interact in their social worlds. Quotes from the women serve to provide context and depth to the findings.

Conception Options of Two Women

Once these couples decided they wanted to parent together, the process of deciding how to bring children into their lives was described as exciting, challenging, and at times exhausting. It involved years of personal reflection and information gathering. Each couple went through their own process of considering a variety of ways of becoming parents including: adoption and fostering, conception with known donors, conception with willing-to-be-known donors, and conception with anonymous donors.

For the couples who contemplated adoption and/or fostering, obstacles presented themselves that caused these mothers to abandon these ideas. Deterrents to proceeding with adoption or fostering, such as the expense (i.e., particularly in the case of overseas adoption), wait-lists, and discrimination against lesbian couples were barriers cited by these mothers that resulted in them considering other, more viable parenting options.

Conceiving their children became an exciting possibility when one or both of the women wanted to experience pregnancy. For the couples who considered known donors, they did so because they felt strongly that they wanted their children to have access to, and possibly a relationship with, the donor should they elect or need to do so in the future. As one mother described:

> When we finally came to the point when we were ready–we thought we would use a known donor because we felt really committed to the idea of the child being able to know the donor–have some kind of a relationship. We were always very clear that we didn't want to co-parent with somebody else.

The couples who wanted to conceive their children with known donors sought either friends or family members who were willing to relinquish their parental rights. Couples approached a number of male friends and asked whether they would be willing to help them conceive their children, have the children know their paternity, and release all of their parental rights. However, a number of concerns emerged as couples worked through the details between themselves and these prospective known donors. What turned out to be "insurmountable barriers" to conceiving children with known donors pertained to concerns related to the donor's future needs or desires for access and/or custody; their children potentially having multiple families and multiple extended families; and the potentially precarious position of non-birth mothers in this type of family constellation.

Couples who were considering conceiving their children with the assistance of male family members asked the non-birth mothers' brothers or cousins to be donors. By involving biologically-related family members of non-birth mothers, these couples were trying to create families in which their children would be biologically related to both mothers. However, a number of complications also arose with family members. For example, some lesbian couples considered whether the donors would be able to separate themselves from wanting some form of involvement in decision-making and/or parenting with their genetic offspring (social nieces and nephews), while other couples wondered how extended family members would view the parenting roles of the non-birth mother, birth mother, and donor. One non-birth mother described her and her partner's concerns in this way:

> It really would have been a pain with my family. I think my family would have always seen my brother as being the father and I would have been the aunt in some weird way and I don't think I would have ever been truly accepted as the parent.

The primary reason couples gave for wanting to conceive with known donor sperm was so that their children would have the potential to meet their donor and/or ask him for more information about himself. As such, another option for the couples who wanted their children to have this potential was to conceive their children with "willing-to-be-known donors." That is, they considered conceiving their children with donors from registered sperm banks who agreed to have their identity known by the children when their offspring reached the age of 18 years. However, a major stumbling block for couples in their consideration of using willing-to-be-known donors was their fear that their children could be hurt if, at the age of 18, they elected to seek out the donor and were unable to contact him, he had passed away, or perhaps even worse–after meeting him they felt disappointed or rejected. One participant described the concerns she had this way:

> More and more people we spoke to said this is a set-up. A set-up in the sense that if the children ask about their genetic father and we say, "Well, when you're 18." So you know, all their life they've built up this idea. Well, what if since he donated he's never told anyone and he goes on to have a wife and family, presuming that he's straight, and suddenly this kid is knocking on his door or what if he finds Jesus and decides that it was wrong–that [the child] is the spawn of the devil, whatever, right? What if he dies or what if he's just not findable?

After very carefully considering the above alternatives, all but one of the couples in the study determined that using an unknown donor was the least risky and most viable option for creating a family together. One couple had the potential to obtain identifying in formation about their donor when their children were 18 years old and had not yet decided how or when to talk to their children about their willing-to-be-known donor. When considering conceiving their children through the use of anonymous donor insemination, these couples reflected on what roles their own fathers played in their lives, how their children may experience being conceived through the use of anonymous donor insemination, and the meaning of raising children without the presence or possibility of paternal involvement or contact. One mother reflected on the challenging and important questions she and her partner faced:

> . . . we got to ask all of the hard philosophical questions, all of them really. What makes a father? What do you need to create a good person? We got to ask and talk with so many people. We have had to work through it all and to talk about all of it and basically, fundamentally what does it take to raise a good person? And we think we can do it just the two of us.

After their children were born, the struggle these moms experienced in making the decision to conceive through the use of anonymous donor insemination quickly dissipated. They felt entitled as the parents of their children and rarely thought about the donor. As one mother stated:

> It's hard not to think that we made them together. We made every decision together. We went to every appointment together. We drove in for the blood tests together. They just couldn't be more ours.

Likewise these mothers noted that with the arrival of their children, extended family members also seemed to forget that there was an anonymous donor involved in their child's conception. One participant described this experience in the following words:

> Once both children were conceived we went forward from there. There was never an issue anymore of the biology of the children. That's long forgotten. I think if you even asked our parents, they'd really have to stop and think about it. Oh yeah, there is a third party, a father out there somewhere but it's so removed now and

it's nice because we are just the parents. And I really don't think it would have been that way if we'd had a known donor.

After their difficult struggles to make the best decisions for themselves and their children, these mothers reported being glad that they chose anonymous donor insemination to conceive their children. One mother described her perception of the advantages of this decision in the following way:

> The benefits–total peace of mind, we're co-parents, nobody is ever going to try and take our child away from us because they can't. We are the legal parents of this person and that is great. I think that is really good. We are protected under the law.

Two Women Parenting

When making choices regarding birth and non-birth mothers, these couples considered how biological connections might or might not influence their roles as mothers. They considered how family life would unfold with one mother biologically related to the children and one mother not sharing a biological or gestational connection.

The couples who chose one woman to be the birth mother of all their children did so for a number of reasons: the non-birth mother did not have a strong desire to experience pregnancy and childbirth; the non-birth mother felt she would love the children irrespective of her genetic relationship to them; and/or the couple wanted their extended family members to treat all their children equally. One couple described their decision to have one partner carry both their children as follows:

> Once we had our first child, I was pretty sure that I didn't want our children having two separate biological mothers, more so from the idea of our families. I really think that that would have been a headache. I think if my partner had given birth to our oldest child and I gave birth to our second child, then our second child would have been in my family and our oldest child would have been in my partner's family and I didn't want to separate them that way. I think the grandparents would have gravitated more towards their biological grandchild.

The belief that children have only one mother is so prevalent in North American culture. So it was not surprising that these couples reported frequently being confronted by questions about who was their child's "real" mother–often leaving the non-gestational mothers feeling invisible. One non-birth mother described her experience of being asked if she or her partner was their daughter's birth mother. She felt people were asking:

> So who is the real mother? That kind of stuff, it just makes me livid. So we hedge about it as much as we can. It depends on who's asking. We have had occasions when we've said we don't feel that's really important. We're both [our child's] mothers. Mostly if people are being kind of offensive about it, that's how we feel. I mean if people are just genuinely sort of intrigued with our process then we tell them.

To mitigate non-birth mothers' feelings of invisibility, these mothers used a variety of strategies including giving the birth and the non-birth mothers names that reflect their equal mothering roles (e.g., mommy and momma), choosing donors that were in some way similar to the non-gestational mothers (e.g., cultural background, physical features), giving their children the last name of the non-birth mothers, not always correcting people who assumed the non-birth mothers were the birth mother, and prior to recent changes in the legal status of the non-gestational mother, ensuring her legal status and entitlement by having her adopt their children.

Couples in which both mothers chose to be birth mothers did so because they both wanted to conceive and carry children, share with each other the experience of carrying children, and/or avoid people slotting them into the categories of biological mother and non-biological mother. These mothers reported being "thrilled" to be able to share the experience of pregnancy with their partners. With both women having the pregnancy and birthing experience, both felt able to more fully appreciate each other's experience. One participant described this in the following words:

> It's just pretty ideal. I can't imagine how many heterosexual women say, "Oh, you know, I'm so envious." I'm so lucky that my partner can appreciate what I was going through and could share the experience.

These mothers also thought that by both being birth mothers, they would be able to avoid people trying to categorize them as the birth and the non-birth mother. In the words of one participant: "Our hope was always that we would each get pregnant and then people wouldn't try to fit us into biological mother and the other mother. We are not the bio and the non-bio mum. We're two mums."

Couples comprised of two women cannot get pregnant by happenstance. Therefore a great deal of planning and preparation reportedly went into these couples' decisions to become parents. They entered into motherhood when they felt their relationships were financially and emotionally secure and when both partners felt fully committed to parenting. These mothers spoke about having put a "lot of thought into deciding if we are going to have a child." They talked about having the "same commitment to the caring role," and about how important it was that their children have "two mums that are basically totally devoted to them." These participants reported "wanting to share parenting." Their commitment to parenting was evident in their subsequent decision-making process regarding the time each spent working outside the home as well as the time each spent parenting.

These mothers described how happy they were to be parenting with another woman. They characterized their relationships as having "shared responsibility" and "full equality in partnering and parenting." These couples talked about enjoying the freedom to negotiate family responsibilities based on preferences, needs of the family, and available time–rather than on sex or gender role prescriptions and expectations. One mother described this process of negotiation as follows:

> If there are jobs to do, laundry or whatever, we'll get to it when we can and it's not specific like it's her's to do the dinner. It is a lot more fun when you can blow up the gender model and then just figure out who likes doing what or who hates it the least amount or who drew the worn card.

Assuming family responsibilities based on negotiation worked for these couples because underlying the negotiations was a commitment to sharing fully the responsibilities of family life. Participants talked about sharing similar values, ideals, and desires in terms of how they wanted their lives with their children to unfold (e.g., time spent in family activities versus individual activities). One mother gave an example of how she and her partner shared the same values regarding their child's needs:

> I couldn't be doing this with a man. There's no way. I just feel so lucky to be with my partner and to be able to negotiate these things

and I think we have it better. I mean we certainly have our roles in the world but it's just different. We just do everything, when it comes to our child, just completely together. It's just equal. So many of the straight mums I know are put in the position of having to choose between their husband or their child's needs and I don't feel that I've ever been in that position because she's a mother too. We haven't gotten into that dynamic where one parent is the expert.

Anonymous Donors/Not Fathers

By the time these parents began the insemination process they had already concluded that they could raise psychologically, socially, and physically healthy and happy children without the presence and availability of fathers. However, the decision to parent without fathers was not a one-time decision that required no further consideration. Rather, couples in this study described an ongoing process of reflection regarding their children's needs for "father figures." Further, these mothers lamented the fact that they did not know what their children would want or need in the future in terms of information about, or contact with, their genetic fathers. That is, these mothers wondered if their children would later be distressed (e.g., during adolescence) about not having fathers in their lives or be upset that their mothers knowingly chose to parent without fathers.

To maximize their children's abilities to cope with not knowing their genetic fathers and to mitigate against any potential challenges their children might experience, these mothers reported doing the following: they made a point of choosing donors with profiles that they anticipated their children will one day feel good about reading; they have been open and honest with their children about their conceptions, their donors, and the absence of fathers in their lives in an age-appropriate manner; and, as dictated by the needs of their children, these mothers have worked towards involving positive male role models in their children's lives.

When choosing their donors, these mothers considered their children's future needs in a variety of ways. The mothers considered a number of issues including choosing donors with profiles that contained a fair bit of information, donors that shared something about themselves in their essays that the mothers thought their children would appreciate reading, and donors who acknowledged the children who might be conceived through their donation. Additionally, these mothers chose the same donor for all of their children.

The mothers who felt it was important for their children to have as much information about the donor and his family and health history as possible, considered donor profiles that contained more information (e.g., baby pictures, adult pictures) rather than less information. For example, one mother described how she and her partner chose their donor on the basis of the amount of information provided by the donor:

> We got a really good deal with the guy we went with because we actually have his picture–when he was a child and as an adult. So our daughter is going to know what he looks like. And she'll have the file. When we chose the donor, we were very conscious of the fact that our daughter is only going to have little bits of information and so we were very conscious of the essays that the donors wrote. We really wanted somebody that made some acknowledgement that there would be children from his donation.

These mothers chose the same donors for all of their children for medical reasons and because they wanted their children to have the same genetic background. They also used the same donor in order to foster a sense of belonging and connection among their children through physically looking alike and from an identity perspective in terms of sharing the experience of coming from the same gene pool. For families in which both women were birth mothers, using the same donor was the biological connection between their children.

These mothers felt strongly that they needed to be open and honest with their children about their unique family situations. They talked openly to their children about their conceptions and their donors, they addressed with their children questions about having two mothers rather than one mom and a father, and they gathered resources to share with their children about people conceived through the use of anonymous donors and living in diverse families.

These mothers described how they worked on being open and matter-of-fact with their two children about their donor. For example, one mother stated:

> We've always talked in terms of the donor. We just call him donor just because it's easier. That's how he's treated. And I'll say things like, you have his hair and I think you must have his hands. So that our daughter can hopefully say, "I've known him for as long as I

can remember." I don't want it to be one day this major shock. It just is going to be her life.

Although these mothers wanted to acknowledge the donor, they did not want to accentuate their children's desire to know or meet their donor. As such, they wanted to distinguish for their children the difference between donors (i.e., genetic fathers) and daddies (i.e., social fathers). In doing so, they attempted to emphasize for their children that being a family with two mothers is wonderful, and that they are not a family without a father; not a family that is deficient. For example, one mother explained how she talked to her son about having two mothers and a "donor daddy":

We've had these talks about where's my daddy? And now he says, "I don't have a daddy. I have a donor daddy." We've been glad to be able to say your daddy is a health professional like mama and he's an artist like me. He sounds like a nice man but he's not a real daddy for you. You have two mummies. He's the one who got you started. So our son knows all about that and it was awkward at first to say it. What we're able to give him is the truth of how he came and how he got started and that he's the best thing that happened to us but we can't give him a "normal family" in quotes. We'll give him a lot of other things but he won't have that and so we've had to say, "No, you don't have a daddy. You have two mums." I think that's one thing that we just need to say again and again is that our families are not made up of this absence. We have so many good things that we can give him.

These women spoke about their desire to have healthy heterosexual and gay male role models involved in the lives of their children. Male family members (e.g., uncles, grandfathers), male friends, and/or male teachers and coaches were typically the men with whom these children spent time. These mothers spoke about wanting to expose their children to men that are "good, kind, loving, intelligent, good citizens," and that represent the "positive role of men in the world." Further, they believed it was important for their children to learn how to comfortably interact with men given that "men make up almost half of the population" and because "a percentage of the rules are made up by men."

The mothers commented on the need for their children not to identify only with the images of men on television or in movies. Thus, they felt strongly that they needed to ensure that the men in their children's lives displayed characteristics they believed were positive. These mothers also noted that if their daughters indicated they wanted to be around men they would attend to this need and try to meet it just as they would for a boy. Thus, these mothers considered the potential importance of healthy male role models in the lives and development of their daughters and their sons.

An important point expressed by these mothers was that they wanted to be responsive to the specific needs of each of their children regarding whether each child wanted to have men in his or her lives as opposed to involving men in their children's lives irrespective of their child's wishes. As one mother described:

> We've started to build a network now that our son is in school. Our son is very male-identified and he has just kind of made it so that we've done more of that because he gravitates towards men. So he's doing it for himself really. He's building those relationships with people–as long as we sort of bring them [men] around.

Families with Lesbian Mothers

Given the heterosexist, genetically-related family model embedded within the fabric of North American society, these mothers were aware that their children would likely experience some forms of discrimination being children of lesbians. For example, they expressed concern about other parents being discriminatory towards their children. In the words of one mother:

> My major concern is having our son prejudiced against because of what other adults think of us. For example, and I am making this up, the lady across the street says, "You can't play with my son because your parents are lesbians." That scares me more than anything because how do you explain to a kid that his best friend isn't allowed to play with him because of who I am. That scares me.

These couples were very aware of their minority status as lesbian families and struggled with finding the language to describe their family roles and family structures. For example, one participant described her struggle to find language to describe her family in the following way:

I'm aware a lot about language and that there's not a language for us and I often feel like we're creating it as we go along. We do not have words that feel comfortable or easy to use yet about our family. We are trying things on for size and biological and non-biological mother are all very cumbersome and unimportant in a way. Just not having a way to speak easily of who we are is a challenge.

To manage being a unique family in a social milieu that privileges heterosexual couples raising children, these mothers made a point of educating and building supportive relationships with extended family members, in their neighborhoods, and in their schools. Couples who felt their extended family members did not support their decision to conceive children as lesbians worked to help them understand prejudice and discrimination against non-heterosexuals. One mother described helping her mother come to a place of acceptance with her decision to become a parent:

I think that if our children have loving friends and family in their lives–that have loved and supported them and their family dynamics and their family structure, then when they do come across somebody who is going to discriminate against them, then they will have the confidence to not care about that or not put too much weight on that because they have gay friends, straight friends, and straight family–relatives that all love and accept them. So if they have enough people in their life, they can draw strength from them. And I said, "You could be a part of the problem or part of the solution. You can be on the other side reacting against us or you can be inside with us and help give love and support to our children so that when they do come across that, they're not going to take it to heart." That they're going to say, "Well, I don't care about what little Joe snotty nose shmuck said at school. My grandparents love me."

Not only did many extended family members arrive at a place of love and acceptance towards these families, these mothers reported that most of their extended family members seem to have forgotten that theirs is a "different" family. That is, these two mother families became just another family in the larger context of their extended family networks.

With the awareness that their children will likely be confronted with questions and prejudices about their family structure, these mothers also chose to educate their children in order to prepare them. They educated their children through talking about their families in matter-of-fact ways, informing them about differences between people and between families, and teaching them to be thoughtful, compassionate people.

Participants were committed to being out as lesbian-led families and families without fathers. They modeled for their children how to talk about their family whenever they were confronted by questions from others. For example, it was not uncommon for these mothers to be asked if the children looked like their father. These mothers responded to those types of questions by saying their children did not have fathers, they have two mothers. They addressed these questions in a direct, clear way, as they wanted their children to learn how to answer these questions when posed to them.

Another way in which these mothers educated their children and prepared them for other people's reactions to their unique family structures and circumstances was by teaching them that there are many types of families. As one mom described, she and her partner believe in "teaching our children that you can have all kinds of families. I have said to her, 'Most families seem to have a mum and a dad, for awhile anyway.' Teaching them that family shifts and changes."

The mothers who thought it was important to educate their children about issues of social justice and gay and lesbian rights either attended or participated in the annual Pride Parade with their children. One mother articulated why it was important for her family to be involved in the parade:

> We were in the Pride March this year for the first time. Our son is just at the age where he can start thinking about it. I said, "We are marching and celebrating because some people used to not like our families or two women who loved each other or two men who loved each other. We have those rights so we celebrate them." And he said, "I'm not going to talk to anybody who doesn't like us." I think he gets it. We're breaking it down for him. And it also hasn't really come up in the schoolyard or any place. It probably will at some point. We're just slowly preparing him.

None of the parents in this study reported that their children had yet experienced any negative comments about their families, given the young age of their children. Therefore, these mothers had not yet educated their children about how to cope with this kind of prejudice directly. However, in anticipation of needing to talk to their children about this issue, participants spoke about being supportive of their children, talking to them, listening to them, working situations out with them, and preparing them for what they might hear as they matured.

Along with education, participants were committed to building a supportive social environment that fostered their children's sense of belonging and that positively reinforced their family structure. The importance of support from extended family members, from neighbors, from school/child-care centre staff, and through connecting to other queer families were all key components these moms felt were important in building a solid foundation for their children.

These mothers chose to live in communities and neighborhoods that valued diversity and in which they felt accepted and felt a sense of belonging. They also felt the need to actively advocate on behalf of their children in schools (and child-care centers). However, the extent to which these mothers advocated varied between couples. Some visited schools and child-care centers prior to their children's attendance to ensure their family structure would be welcomed. Some mothers explicitly asked how their family structure would be included in the curriculum.

Because their families were different from the majority of families, these mothers believed it was also important to consciously create connections with other queer families. One mom described her desire to connect to other families with non-traditional structures in the following way:

> Our son is certainly aware he has two mums and that not everybody does, although he has enough people around him who have the same family situation. We've made a conscious effort to provide him with that so he doesn't feel alone.

By knowing and being friends with other children in similar and diverse family circumstances, these mothers hoped to increase their children's sense of belonging and comfort with their different family structure.

DISCUSSION

The purpose of this study was to investigate the following research question: How do lesbian couples with children conceived through the use of anonymous donor insemination live as, and experience, family? The lesbian-led families in this study were unique in three ways: They had two mothers, their children had anonymous donors and not fathers, and they were headed by a lesbian couple. Four thematic categories emerged from this research which elucidated how these 10 lesbian couples experienced and lived their lives as lesbian mothers with children conceived through the use of anonymous donor insemination.

Given that there is a paucity of research investigating the lives and experiences of lesbian couples with children conceived through the use of anonymous donor insemination, this research provides information for therapists about the process of choosing to conceive children through the use of anonymous donor insemination, as well as living family life with two women parenting, with anonymous donors and not fathers, and with lesbian mothers. However, as a relatively homogenous group of women volunteered for this study, these results do not represent the broad diversity of experiences that likely would be gleaned with a more diverse group of participants.

As noted by many others (e.g., Crawford, 1987; Pies, 1990; Speziale & Gopalakrishna, 2004), mental health professionals working with lesbian couples need to examine their own attitudes and beliefs around lesbianism, lesbians' parenting, third party reproductive technology, and parenting without the presence or availability of fathers. By doing so, it is hoped that therapists who hold discriminatory biases with regard to any of the above issues will choose not to work with this client population. Mental health professionals who do choose to work with this population need to be aware of the ways in which they might implicitly reinforce heterosexist family values (e.g., comparing lesbian-led family experiences with traditional family dynamics and structures); be informed about the issues these couples face (e.g., systemic homophobia, invisibility of non-birth mother roles); and ensure they are able to provide appropriate support, encouragement, empowerment, information, resources, and assistance in working with these couples.

Many of the couples in this study wanted to conceive their children with known donors. However, they were clear that they did not want a third parent in their lives, or the potential legal or social challenges to their parental rights at some point in the future. Consequently they looked for someone (e.g., friends, family member of non-birth mothers) who would relinquish their parental rights and have their paternity known to the child(ren) at some point in the future. A number of obstacles prevented these couples from proceeding with a known donor including: custody and access fears, potential for known donor's extended family interference, and/or potential diminishment of the non-biological mother's role. Therapists can help couples examine the advantages and disadvantages of known or anonymous donor conception, as well as examine the implicit assumptions that underlie the desire for known donors (e.g., the importance of biological connections, especially given the presence of non-birth mothers in these families). To help lesbian couples make fully informed choices, they can refer their clients to legal counsel in order to understand the implications of donor agreements and how well they are recognized in the courts in the face of paternity challenges. Therapists can help women prioritize the criteria by which they make their donor selection.

When deciding that they wanted to conceive their own children, the couples in this study reported going through an exciting, challenging, and at times exhausting process of self-reflection and information gathering. These couples were challenged by other people's (e.g., extended family members) and their own questions about whether it is selfish to bring children into a family that is stigmatized by society. Therapists can help couples examine the assumptions that underlie these issues, confront their fears about what their children might experience, consider what they have to offer children and why they want to raise children, and plan strategies to help clients educate others about these issues (e.g., prejudice is the problem, not lesbians wanting to raise children).

Further, when deciding to conceive their children through the use of anonymous donor insemination, couples in this study examined their beliefs and values about families, the role of men in families and in child development, and how their children might experience living their lives having limited information about their donors and knowing they can never meet their donors. Mental health professionals can help couples investigate each of these issues and assist them in developing ways to manage the challenges of conceiving their children with anonymous donors. For example, therapists can help clients examine how donor selection might mitigate their children's desire to know their donors (e.g., selecting donors with lots of information, choosing the same donor for all of their children).

In Western culture, the idea of family is inexorably linked to biology and to the composition of one mother and one father (Dalton & Bielby, 2000). As such, our society does not recognize non-birth mothers, especially when birth mothers are present in the family. Not surprisingly, in the current study non-birth mothers often felt invisible as mothers. They were asked questions such as, "Who is the 'real' mother?" To manage non-birth mothers' experiences of lacking legitimacy as mothers, the couples in this study employed a number of strategies, from choosing a donor that resembled the non-birth mother to giving the children the non-birth mothers' last name, to having the non-biological mother legally adopt their child. Mental health professionals can help lesbian couples become aware of, and prepare to deal with, instances when non-birth mothers might feel less legitimate as mothers than birth mothers. Therapists can also assist couples by referring them for legal counsel so that they can become informed about the issues salient to lesbian couples who choose to conceive children together (e.g., second parent adoptions, marriage, death of birth mother).

Participants in this study were committed to being open and honest with their children about their conceptions, donors (i.e., genetic fathers), and "daddies" (i.e., social fathers). Therefore, mental health professionals can help lesbian couples role-play ways to talk to their children, educate mothers about child development and the necessity of using age-appropriate language and concepts, and refer them to appropriate resources. Further, as couples in this study differed in the manner in which they discussed the donor (e.g., some mothers mentioned the donor regularly whereas others preferred to wait for the children to ask for information), therapists can help clients weigh the pros and cons of the ways in which they want to incorporate this information into their children's lives and the timing and age-appropriateness of the disclosure of this information. Clients might also benefit from reading the article by Blumenthal (1990) entitled, *Scrambled Eggs and Seed Daddies: Conversations with My Son,* which relays how the author talked to her son about being conceived through the use of donor insemination.

As noted by Clunis and Green (1995), terminology commonly used to describe families does not always fit for lesbian-led families. The mothers in this study talked about not having the language to describe their families adequately and easily. For example, the terms "non-birth" and "non-biological" mother were found to be cumbersome and minimizing ways to identify co-mothers and their roles. Mental health professionals can assist clients in finding the language that feels comfortable to them and that appropriately reflects their roles within their families. Also, mental health professionals can refer clients to Lev's (2004) *The Complete Lesbian & Gay Parenting Guide,* which provides information about language usage with children at varying stages of development.

The mothers in this study reported that support from extended family members and members of the straight and queer communities helped them feel confident and validated as parents and, as such, better able to deal with challenges pertaining to homophobia and heterosexism. Mental health professionals can work with couples to develop this support through helping mothers prepare to educate people around them (e.g., extended family members), choose to reside in neighborhoods that value diversity, and build friendship networks both for themselves and their children with other lesbian-led and queer families.

Participants wanted to impress upon their children the belief that their family is not lacking in any way because fathers were not present and available. To minimize the risk of their children incorporating this message, these mothers employed a variety of strategies [e.g., changing Father's Day into Parent's Day, teaching children there are many types of families, emphasizing what they have (i.e., two moms), not what is absent (e.g., social fathers)]. Thus, therapists can help lesbian couples reflect on the ways in which they might unconsciously be imparting this message to their children and ways in which they can model for, and teach their children to experience, their family as complete.

The mothers in the present study were aware that their children might at some point in their lives be conflicted about not having social fathers. Thus, these mothers employed a variety of strategies to help their children (e.g., choosing donors whose profiles they believed their children would appreciate reading). Mental health professionals can help couples explore all the potential pros and cons related to donor choice in terms of child and family needs.

Limitations

While important, the extent to which these findings apply to or resonate with the experiences of other lesbian-led families may be limited for a number of reasons. Similar to the studies by other researchers who have investigated lesbian-led families (e.g., Gartrell et al., 1996; Patterson et al., 1998), participants in this study were a relatively homogeneous group. These mothers were self-reflective, well-educated, thoughtful, mainly of Western Europe descent, and relatively affluent. Thus, how well the experiences of these couples resonate with couples from other cultures, and couples with less education and economic and social resources, is unknown.

The couples who participated in this study live in or near a large Canadian city in which same-sex marriages and second parent adoptions are legal, and in which gay and lesbian communities are noteworthy. Although homophobia, heterosexism, and violence against gays and lesbians prevail, gay and lesbian legal and social rights are developing. Couples residing in other geographic locations (e.g., in rural communities, other countries) may live in very different social and legal contexts.

It is also important to note that this was a cross-sectional study–a mere snapshot of how family was lived and experienced by these mothers of young children. Therefore, how the process of family life continued to unfold over time for these families was not captured in this study. Further research is necessary to capture these changes and to elucidate the experiences of lesbian mothers and their children over time.

REFERENCES

Alexander, C. J. (1997). Gay and lesbian parenting: A unique opportunity for sexual minority research. *Journal of Gay & Lesbian Social Services, 7*(1), 87-91.

Alldred, P. (1998). Making a mockery of family life? Lesbian mothers in the British media. *Journal of Lesbian Studies, 2,* 9-21.

Arnup, K. (1998). "Does the word LESBIAN mean anything to you?" Lesbians raising daughters. In S. Abbey & A. O'Reilly (Eds.), *Redefining motherhood: Changing identities and patterns* (pp. 59-68). Toronto: Second Story Press.

Arnup, K. (1997). In the family way: Lesbian mothers in Canada. In M. Luxton (Ed.), *Feminism and families: Critical policies and changing practices* (pp. 80-97). Halifax: Fernwood Publishing.

Blumenthal, A. (1990). Scrambled eggs and seed daddies: Conversations with my son. *Empathy, 2(2),* 45-48.

Bos, H. M. W., van Balen, F., & van den Boom, D. C. (2004). Experience of parenthood, couple relationship, social support, and child-rearing goals in planned lesbian mother families. *Journal of Child Psychology and Psychiatry, 45*(4), 755-764.

Boyd, P. (1998). Solutions to infertility: Even the simplest medical answers raise troubling ethical questions for Catholics. *Counseling and Values, 33,* 234-238.

Brewaeys, A., Devroey, P., Helmerhorst, F. M., Van Hall, E. V., & Ponjaert, I. (1995). Lesbian mothers who conceived after donor insemination: A follow-up study. *Human Reproduction, 10*(10), 2731-2735.

Chan, R. W., Brooks, R. C., Raboy, B., & Patterson, C. J. (1998). Division of labor among lesbian and heterosexual parents: Associations with children's adjustment. *Journal of Family Psychology, 12*(3), 402-419.

Clarke, V. (2002). Sameness and difference in research on lesbian parenting. *Journal of Community & Applied Social Psychology, 12,* 210-222.

Clunis, D. M., & Green, G. D. (1995). *The lesbian parenting book: A guide to creating families and raising children.* Seattle: Seal Press.

Crawford, S. (1987). Lesbian Families: Psychological stress and the family-building process. In Boston Lesbian Psychologies Collective (Ed.) *Lesbian psychologies: Explorations and challenges* (pp.195-214). Urbana: University of Illinois Press.

Dalton, S. E., & Bielby, D. D. (2000). "That's our kind of constellation." Lesbian mothers negotiate institutionalized understandings of gender within the family. *Gender & Society, 14*(1), 36-61.

Denzin, N. K. (2001). *Interpretive interactionism, Vol. 16. Applied social research methods series* (2nd ed.). Newbury Park: Sage.

Denzin, N. K. (1989). *Interpretive interactionism, Vol. 16. Applied social research methods series.* Newbury Park: Sage.

Dunne, G. A. (2000). Opting into motherhood: Lesbians blurring the boundaries and transforming the meaning of parenthood and kinship. *Gender & Society, 14*(1), 36-61.

Englert, Y. (1994). Artificial insemination of single women and lesbian women with donor insemination. *Human Reproduction, 9*(11), 1969-1977.

Evans, B. K. (1990). Mothering as a lesbian issue. *Journal of Feminist Family Therapy, 2*(1), 43-52.

Falk, P. J. (1994). The gap between psychosocial assumptions and empirical research in lesbian-mother child custody cases. In A. E. Gottfried & A. W. Gottfried (Eds.), *Redefining families: Implications for children's development* (pp. 131-156). New York: Plenum Press.

Gartrell, N., Banks, A., Hamilton, J., Reed, N., Hamilton, J., Rodas, C., & Deck, A. (2000). The National Lesbian Family Study: 3. Interviews with mothers of five-year-olds. *American Journal of Orthopsychiatry, 70*(4), 542-549.

Gartrell, N., Banks, A., Hamilton, J., Reed, N., Bishop, H., & Rodas, C. (1999). The National Lesbian Family study: 2. Interviews with mothers of toddlers. *American Journal of Orthopsychiatry, 69*(3), 362-369.

Gartrell, N., Hamilton, J., Banks, A., Mosbacher, D., Reed, N., Sparks, C. H., & Bishop, H. (1996). The National Lesbian Family study: 1. Interviews with prospective mothers. *American Journal of Orthopsychiatry, 66*(2), 272-281.

Golombok, S. (1999). New family forms: Children raised in solo mother families, lesbian mother families, and in families created by assisted reproduction. In L. Balter & C. S.Tamis-LeMonda (Eds.), *Child psychology: A handbook of contemporary issues* (pp. 429-446). Philadelphia: Psychology Press.

Golombok, S., Perry, B., Burston, A., Murray, C., Mooney-Somers, J., Stevens, M., & Golding, J. (2003). Children with lesbian parents: A community study. *Developmental Psychology, 39*(1), 20-33.

Golombok, S., Spencer, A., & Rutter, M. (1983). Children in lesbian and single-parent households: Psychosexual and psychiatric appraisal. *Journal of Child Psychology & Psychiatry and Allied Disciplines, 24*(4), 551-572.

Golombok, S., & Tasker, F. (1996). Do parents influence the sexual orientation of their children? Findings from a longitudinal study of lesbian families. *Developmental Psychology, 32*(1), 3-11.

Green, R., Mandel, J. B., Hotvedt, M. E., Gray, J., & Smith, L. (1986). Lesbian mothers and their children: A comparison with solo parent heterosexual mothers and their children. *Archives of Sexual Behavior, 15*(2), 167-184.

Haimes, E., & Weiner, K. (2000). Everybody's got a dad... Issues for lesbian families in the management of donor insemination. *Sociology of Health and Illness, 22*(4), 477-499.

Hare, J. (1994). Concerns and issues faced by families headed by a lesbian couple. *Families in Society: The Journal of Contemporary Human Services, 75*(1), 27-35.

Hoeffer, B. (1981). Children's acquisition of sex-role behavior in lesbian-mother families. *American Journal of Orthopsychiatry, 51*(3), 536-544.

Huggins, S. L. (1989). A comparative study of self-esteem of adolescent children of divorced lesbian mothers and divorced heterosexual mothers. In F. W. Bozett (Ed.), *Homosexuality and the family* (123-135). New York: Harrington Park Press.

Jacob, M. C., Klock, S. C., & Maier, D. (1999). Lesbian couples as therapeutic donor insemination recipients: Do they differ from other patients? *Journal of Obstetric Gynecology, 20,* 203-215.

Javaid, G. A. (1993). The children of homosexual and heterosexual single mothers. *Child Psychiatry and Human Development, 23*(4), 235-248.

Kaufman, M., & Dundas, S. (1995). Directions for research about lesbian families. In K. Arnup (Ed.), *Lesbian parenting: Living with pride and prejudice* (pp. 166-176). Charlottetown, PEI: gynergy.

Kirpatrick, M. J. (1990). Homosexuality and parenting. In J. Spurlock & C. B. Robinowitz (Eds.), *Women's progress: Promises and problems* (pp. 205-222). New York: Plenum Press.

Kirpatrick, M., Smith, C., & Roy, R. (1981). Lesbian mothers and their children: A comparative survey. *American Journal of Orthopsychiatry, 51*(3), 545-551.

Kweskin, S. L., & Cook, A. S. (1982). Heterosexual and homosexual mothers' self-described sex-role behavior and ideal sex-role behavior in children. *Sex Roles, 8*(9), 967-975.

Lempert, N. B., & DeVault, M. (2000). Guest editors' introduction: Special issue on emergent and reconfigured forms of family life. *Gender & Society, 14*(1), 6-10.

Lev, A. I. (2004). *The complete lesbian & gay parenting guide.* New York: Berkley Books.

Miller, J. A., Jacobson, R. B., & Bigner, J. J. (1982). The child's home environment for lesbian versus heterosexual mothers: A neglected area of research. *Journal of Homosexuality, 7*(1), 49-56.

Mucklow, B. M., & Phelan, G. K. (1979). Lesbian and traditional mothers' responses to adult response to child behavior and self-concept. *Psychological Reports, 44*(3), 880-882.

Nelson, F. (1996). *Lesbian motherhood: An exploration of Canadian lesbian families.* Toronto: University of Toronto.

O'Connell, A. (1992). Voices from the heart: The developmental impact of a mother's lesbianism on her adolescent children. *Smith College Studies in Social Work, 63*(3), 281-299.

Osborne, J. W. (1990). Some similarities and differences among phenomenological and other methods of psychological qualitative research. *Canadian Psychology/ Psychologie Canadienne, 35*(2), 167-189.

Patterson, C. J. (1997). Children of lesbian and gay parents. *Advances in Clinical Child Psychology, 19,* 235-282.

Patterson, C. J. (1996). Lesbian and gay parents and their children. In R. C. Savin-Williams & K. M. Cohen (Eds.), *The lives of lesbian, gays, and bisexuals: Children to adults* (pp. 274-304). Orlando: Harcourt Brace College.

Patterson, C. J. (1995a). Lesbian mothers, gay fathers, and their children. In A. R. D'Augelli & C. J. Patterson (Eds.), *Lesbian, gay, and bisexual identities over the lifespan* (pp. 262-292). New York: Oxford University Press.

Patterson, C. J. (1995b). Families of the lesbian baby boom: Parents' division of labor and children's adjustment. *Developmental Psychology, 31*(1), 115-123.

Patterson, C. J. (1994). Children of the lesbian baby boom: Behavioral adjustment, self concepts, and sex role identity. In B. Greene & G. M. Herek (Eds.), *Contemporary perspectives on lesbian and gay psychology: Theory, research, and clinical applications, Vol. 1* (pp. 156-175).Thousand Oaks: Sage.

Patterson, C. J., Hurt, S., & Mason, C. D. (1998). Families of the lesbian baby boom: Children's contact with grandparents and other adults. *American Journal of Orthopsychiatry, 68*(3), 390-399.

Pies, C. A. (1990). Lesbians and the choice to parent. In F. W. Bozett & M. B. Sussman (Eds.), *Homosexuality and family relations* (pp. 137-154). New York: Harrington Park Press.

Pies, C. (1988). *Considering parenthood.* San Francisco: Spinsters Ink.

Pies, C. (1987). Considering parenthood: Psychosocial issues for gay men and lesbians choosing alternative fertilization. In F. W. Bozett (Ed.), *Gay and lesbian parents* (pp. 165-173). New York: Praegar.

Polikoff, N. D. (1992). Lesbian mothers, lesbian families: Legal obstacles, legal challenges. In D. J. Maggiore (Ed.), *Lesbians and child custody: A casebook* (pp. 229-237). New York: Garland Publishing.

Pollack, S. (1992). Lesbian mothers: A lesbian-feminist perspective on research. In D. J. Maggiore (Ed.), *Lesbians and child custody: A casebook* (pp. 219-228). New York: Garland Publishing.

Riley, C. (1988). American kinship: A lesbian account. *Feminist Issues, 8,* 75-94.

Shore, E. A. (1996). What kind of lesbian is a mother? *Journal of Feminist Family Therapy, 8*(3), 45-62.

Speziale, B., & Gopalakrishna, V. (2004). Social support and function of nuclear families headed by lesbian couples. *Affilia, 19*(2), 174-184.

Stacey, J., & Biblarz, T. J. (2001). (How) does the sexual orientation of parents matter? *American Sociological Association, 66*(2), 159-183.

Stein, T. S. (1988). Homosexuality and new family forms: Issues in psychotherapy. *Psychiatric Annals, 18*(1), 12-20.

Stevens, M., Perry, B., Burston, A., Golombok, S., & Golding, J. (2003). Openness in lesbian-mother families regarding mother's sexual orientation and child's conception by donor insemination. *Journal of Reproductive and Infant Psychology, 21*(4), 347-362.

Tasker, F., & Golombok, S. (1995). Adults raised as children in lesbian families. *American Journal of Orthopsychiatry, 65*(2), 203-215.

Thorne, B. (1992). Feminism and the family: Two decades of feminist thought. In B. Thorne (Ed.), *Rethinking the family: Some feminist questions* (pp. 3-26). Boston: Northeastern University Press.

Tulchinsky, K. X. (1999, May 8). Two moms, better than one? Staking claim to Mother's Day: Once we decided which one of us would bear the child, our little family adventure was underway. *Vancouver Sun,* pp. E5. Retrieved August 21, 2000 from the World Wide Web: http://halfway.library.ubc.ca/cgiubc/webspirscnews.cgi? sp.usernumber.p=839672&url=yes&sp.nextform=show1rec.htm&sp.dbid.p=C69

A%2CC69B%2CC69C%2CC69D&sp.url.p=I(C69A)J(0000135454)&sp.record.source.p = _HOTLINK

Vanfraussen, K., Ponjaert-Kristoffersen, I., & Brewaeys, A. (2003). Family functioning in lesbian families created by donor insemination. *American Journal of Orthopsychiatry, 73*(1), 78-90.

Wilson, C. M. (2000). The creation of motherhood: Exploring the experiences of lesbian co-mothers. *Journal of Feminist Family Therapy, 12*(1), 21-44.

doi:10.1300/J086v18n01_01

Redefining the Nuclear Family:
An Exploration of Resiliency
in Lesbian Parents

A. Cassandra Golding

SUMMARY. During a two-month period, in-depth semi-structured interviews were conducted with single and partnered lesbians who had children either through adoption, artificial insemination, or a previous relationship. Home environment stability and mothers' psychological well-being seemed to influence children's self-esteem and overall well-being according to mothers' self-report. Age of children when mothers "came out" to them and the degree to which children were comfortable discussing their parents' sexuality seemed to play a key role in the overall satisfaction of children as they matured. This researcher used qualitative methods to explore the adversities and coping methods of fourteen

Address correspondence to: A. Cassandra Golding, Department of Psychology, University of Rhode Island, Kingston, RI 02881(E-mail: cgolding@mail.uri.edu).

This research was conducted while the author was an undergraduate at Saint Mary's College of California under the supervision of Dr. Nancy Struthers. The author is grateful for the support of Dr. Struthers, the willingness and courage of the participants and constructive criticism on revisions of this manuscript from the reviewers and editors of *Journal of Feminist Family Therapy*. The author presented portions of this work at the Sigma Xi Scientific Research Society poster session at Saint Mary's College of California, the 11th Annual University of Rhode Island Symposium on Gay, Lesbian, Bisexual, Transgender and Questioning Issues and the Second Annual International Conference on Social Science Research.

[Haworth co-indexing entry note]: "Redefining the Nuclear Family: An Exploration of Resiliency in Lesbian Parents." Golding, A. Cassandra. Co-published simultaneously in *Journal of Feminist Family Therapy* (The Haworth Press, Inc.) Vol. 18, No. 1/2, 2006, pp. 35-65; and: *Lesbian Families' Challenges and Means of Resiliency: Implications for Feminist Family Therapy* (ed: Anne M. Prouty Lyness) The Haworth Press, Inc., 2006, pp. 35-65. Single or multiple copies of this article are available for a fee from The Haworth Document Delivery Service [1-800-HAWORTH, 9:00 a.m. - 5:00 p.m. (EST). E-mail address: docdelivery@haworthpress.com].

lesbian parents interviewed, and assessed the ability of these women to be effective parents based on the strength and resiliency exemplified. A thorough literature review includes: History of the same-sex marriage and family movement, adoption options, as well as the history of same-sex parenting research and current research concerning same-sex parenting. doi:10.1300/J086v18n01_02 *[Article copies available for a fee from The Haworth Document Delivery Service: 1-800-HAWORTH. E-mail address: <docdelivery@haworthpress.com> Website: <http://www.HaworthPress.com>*

KEYWORDS. Lesbian, parenting, sexual orientation, same-sex, family, adoption

INTRODUCTION

In the past two decades, the conventional family has undergone significant changes. The nuclear family is no longer exclusively defined as two opposite sex, married parents with two biological children. Rather, our definition of the nuclear family has expanded to include single parents, mixed families, step-families, families with biological children, adoptive children, grandchildren, nieces, nephews, foster children . . . so many ways we have come to define a family. Perhaps the most controversial of these reconceptualizations of the nuclear family is the inclusion of gay and lesbian families.

This new millennium brings with it the struggles of lesbian and gay male couples and individuals as they strive for equal acknowledgment and family rights. The social definition of marriage and the constitutional right to marry have been denied, re-founded and manipulated throughout the centuries. There was a time when women were their husband's property and interracial marriages were illegal. Similarly, same-sex couple rights activists are fighting to attain the same equality that has historically been extended to women and ethnic minorities by the courts and in various social arenas. In this way marriage has been evaluated before, and yet again, the definition of marriage is under debate (Sullivan, 1996). This epitomizes one of the most extraordinary and adversely opposed junctures in the patterns of the Western family. Thus, it is no surprise that the psychological research concerning the issues surrounding gay and lesbian families has become a fervent series of developments that provoke ardent divisions. Unlike most, the consequences of this research impinge on public policies concerning marriage and family, and these are significantly influenced by Western culture's most vigorously held convictions about gender, sexuality, and parenthood.

It follows from these societal ideals, that although research suggests that children of gays and lesbians grow up just as healthy, happy, and "normal" as children of heterosexual families, stigmatization continues to plague gays and lesbians as these parents fight for the rights to enjoy their unique families, fight for recognition in public policy and struggle to receive the legal benefits afforded to other families. This stigmatization and, particularly, doubts concerning the ability of gays and lesbians to be fit parents have necessitated that gays and lesbians call upon a profound strength, a unique resiliency in their parenting which shelters their children from hardship, yet fights adversity simultaneously.

While the research defending the parenting abilities of gays and lesbians is abundant, little research exists that focuses specifically on the resilient characteristics exemplified by these unique parents. Further, even fewer researchers have evaluated the coping methods employed by gay and lesbian parents as they fight for social survival in a culture that perceives gay and lesbian parenting as an oxymoron: raising children, a traditionally heterosexual role, is now being assumed by a non-traditional sexual minority (Siegenthaler & Bigner, 2000). The purpose of this manuscript is to review the literature including the history of the same-sex marriage and family movement; acknowledge the numerous steps required for lesbians to become parents and/or legally have rights to the non-biological children they raise; evaluate what it means to be an effective parent in this society; explore the adversities and coping methods of the sample of women interviewed; and discuss the ability of lesbians to be effective parents based on the strength and resiliency they exemplify. Following this literature review, the author reports on the findings of a small qualitative study in which she evaluated resiliency in lesbian parenting as a way of contributing to this literature.

LITERATURE REVIEW

Brief History of the Movement for Same-Sex Marriage

These issues by no means exist in a vacuum; in fact the development of this newly defined family has been evaluated across the world. As the last millennium came to a close, France established registered partnerships across the nation. Denmark included same-sex couples in child custody rights and has now given these couples full marriage rights. Various forms of civil unions have been established in Germany, Portugal, Israel, the United Kingdom, and New Zealand. Most significantly, The Netherlands in 2000 emerged as the first nation to make reality what was inevitable after Dutch legislatures elected dramatically to extend the fundamental rights of legal marriage to gay and lesbian couples (Human Rights Campaign, 2006). In 2002, Newfoundland and Labrador granted gays and lesbians the right to adopt and Sweden entered legislation to do the same (Kirk, 2005). In 2003, Belgium became the second country in the world to grant legal marriage for gays and lesbians although adoption rights were not approved. In June of 2005 Spain was added to the list as the third country in the world to allow gays and lesbians the benefits of full marriage rights. Just over a month later, Canadian federal law legalized same-sex marriage on July 20th, 2005 after eight of the provinces and one territory had done so for their respective jurisdictions starting in 2003. The Constitutional Court of South Africa on December 1st, 2005 also elected to legalize same-sex marriage, extending equal rights to same-sex couples and their families in 2006 (Human Rights Campaign, 2006).

In the United States, on April 25th, 2000, Vermont became the first state to legally recognize same-sex couples when governor, Howard Dean, signed a civil union bill. At midnight on May 17th, 2004 Cambridge, Massachusetts started accepting marriage license applications from same-sex couples with over 600 couples' applications received in one day across the state, making Massachusetts the first state to offer same-sex couples marriage licenses recognized statewide after three years of court battles. In October of 2005, Connecticut began to accept same-sex civil union licenses as well.

Despite these significant strides in the movement for equal marriage and family rights for same-sex couples, many other attempts to do the same by same-sex couples and allied politicians in several other states have been stifled. In February of 2004, the city of San Francisco issued marriage licenses to over 2,000 gay and lesbian couples in only a few days. However, by the next November, the California Supreme Court ruled to invalidate the more than 4,000 licenses issued by the city. Similarly, in February of 2004 Sandoval County, New Mexico issued marriage licenses to same-sex couples and the New Mexico attorney general nullified these licenses within three days. In Oregon's Multnomah County, the almost 3,000 same-sex marriages performed in April of 2004 were revoked by the Oregon State Supreme Court the following

April. Although California's state Senate and state House voted to legalize same-sex couple marriage in September of 2005, Governor Arnold Schwarzenegger vetoed the bill that same month. Currently, 13 states: Arkansas, Georgia, Kentucky, Michigan, Mississippi, Montana, North Dakota, Ohio, Oklahoma, Oregon, Utah, and most recently Kansas and Texas uphold state constitutional amendments banning marriage rights for same-sex couples (Human Rights Campaign, 2006).

Composition of Gay and Lesbian Families

Approximately 25 million U.S. citizens are gay or lesbian. Six to 14 million children have at least one biological gay or lesbian parent (Sullivan, 1995), and eight to 10 million children are being raised in gay and lesbian households (Harvard, 1990). According to the 2000 Census,[1] one in three lesbian couples (34.3 percent) and one in five gay male couples (22.3 percent) are raising children under the age of 18 years. Surprisingly, the South encompasses the largest population of lesbian (36.1 percent) and gay male couples (23.9 percent) with kids. The Midwest follows with 34.7 and 22.9 percent, respectively, then the West for lesbian couples and the Northeast for gay male couples. Mississippi, South Dakota, Utah and Texas have the most lesbian couples raising children with 43.8 percent, 42.3 percent each, and 40.9 percent respectively. Similarly, gay male couples raising children are most prevalent in South Dakota (33 percent), Mississippi (31 percent), and Idaho and Utah (30 percent each) (Bennett & Gates, 2003).

Gays and lesbians have for years used several methods of becoming parents including public adoption, private adoption, international adoption, artificial insemination, previous marriage, and sperm donors. No matter what the method for conception is, however, if both partners want legal rights to the child, the non-biological parent must legally adopt (Bigner, 2000; Executive, 2002). One of the fundamental arguments against same-sex parenting is a seemingly lack of stability (Bigner, 2000; Patterson, 2004). However, the 2000 Census documents that actually gay and lesbian couples are more than twice as likely (41.1 percent) to be involved in a long-term relationship (lasting more than five years) than are unmarried heterosexual couples with children (19.1 percent). As homeownership is also considered indicative of family stability, the rate of homeownership among gay and lesbian couples (64.3 percent) which far exceeds that of unmarried couples (45.4 percent) according to the 2000 Census, is further evidence of gay and lesbian parents' capabilities to create a safe, healthy, and stable home environment for the children they raise (Bennett & Gates, 2003).

Adoption

In 1999, approximately 547,000 United States children were in foster care and 117,000 were available for adoption, but in 1997 there were only enough qualified parents (single parents included) for 20% of these children (Sullivan, 1995). Currently, 21 states have allowed same-sex couple adoption including: Alaska, California, Colorado, Connecticut, Hawaii, Illinois, Massachusetts, New Jersey, New York, Ohio, Rhode Island, Vermont, Washington, and the District of Columbia, although Florida and New Hampshire have assumed laws that specifically bar gays and lesbians from adopting (Kirk, 2005). In 1994, Congress put into effect the Multiethnic Placement Act (MEPA) which bars any federally assisted agency from denying any individual the opportunity to become a foster or adoptive parent based solely on race, color or national origin. However, only California and New York have established laws that protect against discrimination specifically toward gays and lesbians (Executive, 2002).

Methods of Adoption

Many gays and lesbians, either single or part of a couple, are often treated like second-class citizens by adoptive agencies, finding themselves at the bottom of an unspoken hierarchy which favors white, middle-class, heterosexual couples. As a result, gays and lesbians are often only able to adopt those kids who are seen as less preferred, those children who are older, children of color, part of sibling groups, or those with physical, mental or emotional handicaps (HRC, 2006; Executive, 2002). Psychologist April Martin, author of *The Lesbian and Gay Parent Handbook* (1993), suggests that in order to adopt younger and physically, mentally and emotionally healthier children, same-sex couples use private, independent, or international adoption methods. These methods, however, can be two-thirds more expensive and exclude, therefore, those couples with lower socioeconomic status (Cost, 2000).

There are two forms of traditional adoption open to gay and lesbian couples, private-placement and public agency. The adoption process is long and tedious. It usually involves several applications, petitions, court proceedings, legal paper work, and a thorough home study by social workers who may or may not be open to gay or lesbian parenting.

All adoption processes aim to attend to the best interest of the child (Hollinger, 2000).

Private-placement includes private agency adoption, independent adoption, and international adoption in which state agency involvement is not necessary. Private adoption agencies often provide pre-adoption parent education and post-adoption services in addition to obtaining all the legal material and making all the necessary legal arrangements for adoptive parents. These services will cost between $4,000 and $30,000 (Cost, 2000). The home study fees may be waived or greatly reduced for the adoption of a special-needs child. Private agencies determine their own criteria for prospective adoptive parents; thus, they may consider age, religion, fertility status, marital status, and sexual orientation. Further, some agencies choose to present gay or lesbian adoptive parents as single adults living with another single adult who will share in child-care responsibilities and, thus, disregard sexual orientation (Sullivan, 1995; Martin, 2000). Independent adoption is either a "direct placement" by a biological parent to adoptive parents or a placement that involves an intermediary agent, like an attorney, bringing the birth and adoptive parents together. These costs can be about the same as private adoption fees ranging from $8,000 to $30,000 (Cost, 2000).

International adoption refers to the adoption of children from foreign countries by U.S. citizens and is usually arranged through adoption agencies. Because cultural standards dictate foreign country adoption laws as well as government interpretation of *the best interest of a child*, religious, conservative and developing countries are rarely receptive to gay and lesbian couples. Consequently, agencies are usually only able to grant parental rights to one parent, requiring the other partner to adopt through the U.S. state public agency system as a second-parent (Hollinger, 2000; Sullivan, 1995). Nevertheless, gay and lesbian parents-to-be may prefer this method of adoption because almost 90 percent of children adopted internationally are less than five years old, and almost half are infants, compared to two percent of the children adopted from foster care (Statistical, 1998). However, costs can be from $7,000 to $25,000 not including the fees for a second parent adoption (Cost, 2000).

Public agency adoption refers to the adoption of a foster child in the care of the state who is placed for adoption by a foster care agency. This form of adoption can cost anywhere from nothing to $2,500 depending on the agency and the circumstances (Cost, 2000). In addition, a gay or lesbian individual wishing to adopt their partner's biological or adoptive child must proceed through a second-parent adoption. Although this only requires that a legal guardian give his/her consent, some state courts have found reasons to prohibit second-parent adoptions to gays and lesbians despite the same-sex orientation of the present custodian (Hollinger, 2000). This process is essentially the same as a public agency adoption and will cost a couple up to $2,500 (Cost, 2000).

History of Gay and Lesbian Parenting Research

When compared to their heterosexual counterparts, significant research has shown little differences in overall mental health or approaches to child rearing for lesbians. Although little research has been conducted concerning gay fathers, the research that does exist shows gay males to be just as fit as any male to love and care for a child (Patterson, 1995). Organized research on gay and lesbian adults began in the late 1950s. Research on the children of gays and lesbians was first published in 1978, but most research has only been published in the last 10 years. Methodology in this area of study has been challenging and is often criticized for deriving general conclusions based on small samples, lack of statistical significance, reliance on self-report data, and lack of longitudinal data. As with any research of a controversial nature, the data is difficult to collect and finding subjects is complicated, time consuming, and requires a delicate balance of courage and sensitivity (Patterson, 1994a).

Although considerable efforts have been made by progressive researchers such as Bigner (2000), Siegenthaler and Bigner (2000), and Miller, Jacobsen, and Bigner (1981), little data is available on gay male fathers mostly due to the lack of gay male fathers who have sole custody of children from previous heterosexual relationships. Siegenthaler and Bigner (2000) explain that gay male fathers and lesbian mothers seem to experience similar desires to be parents; however, the realities of their parenting experiences may differ considerably given that the parental role is often more a central focus for lesbian mothers as a result of their sole custody of children from past heterosexual relationships. Thus, most studies concerning gay and lesbian parenting concentrate on lesbian mothers (Bigner, 2000; Miller et al., 1981).

Effective Parenting

Effective parenting is essential to the success of any society. Children must be raised in homes where they receive love and affection, security and stability. As the number of children in need of homes grows and more and more single parents continue to head households, the issues surrounding parenting become increasingly prevalent (Nelson, 1996, 1999). The concept of gays and lesbians becoming parents presents society-at-large with an "enigma in that they [gay and lesbian parents] represent a conflicting, contradictory dual identity that pits myths and stereotypes about both heterosexuality and homosexuality against one another" (Siegenthaler & Bigner, 2000, p. 74). Dominant society has presumed that parenting is a role appropriate only for heterosexuals; thus, gay and lesbian parents baffle the general population and represent a paradox that is fueled by cultural misinterpretations about the lifestyles and parenting abilities of gays and lesbians. Traditionally, gay and lesbian parents have been perceived as incapable of providing a healthy environment in which to raise healthy children and, further, unqualified to serve as favorable role models for those maturing children.

Despite an abundance of research that negates these societal ideations, homophobia and bias have created a hostile and unsupportive environment for lesbian mothers and gay male fathers. Undoubtedly, gay and lesbian families are often the target of prejudice, which can turn adjudicators, lawmakers, authorities, and the public against them (Nelson, 1996). In attempting to negotiate the realities of two contradicting roles as gay or lesbian and a parent, gay and lesbian families must contentiously govern their child's social development amidst a constant environment of contradiction (Wahler & Smith, 1999). The negative consequences associated with this contradictory lifestyle often encourage secrecy with community agencies such as schools and employers which can, in turn, socially isolate these already marginalized families and deprive children of valuable social resources, support and networks (Siegenthaler & Bigner, 2000).

Societal beliefs about gays and lesbians are generally not based on personal experience, but rather on culturally transmitted stereotypes (Patterson, 1992). Thus, the gay and lesbian parents who dare to defy this culture-wide phenomenon must, on the one hand, have a deep, passionate desire to raise a child, love a child, and fully live the profound interdependency that only a child-parent relationship can embody. On the other hand, in order to do this well, these parents, just by their shear courage, must inherently possess incredible personal strength, a strong sense of self, ability not only to protect and make sense of an unaccepting world for themselves, but for their child as well. In a practical sense, lesbian mothers must confront the opposing significance society has placed upon their double role as a woman whose ultimate purpose in life is to bear children, and a lesbian, who is not suited to do so.

April Martin (1993) has pointed out that gay and lesbian families have unique strengths: the ability to accept differences, to understand what it is like to be in the minority, to demonstrate flexible gender roles, to be open about sexuality with children who have been sexually abused, and to understand the special needs of gay or lesbian children that make them excellent, and in some cases, the best homes for certain children. The coping skills and unique strategies employed by gay and lesbian parents are indicative of powerful resiliency that allows the gay and lesbian parenting movement to thrive and, further, allows these parents to live with pride despite many odds and constant obstacles.

The Resilient Individual

Resiliency is a subjective term. Depending on who you ask and who you are referring to, resiliency can include an array of definitions. In its simplest form resiliency is emotional strength. However, it is so much more and the consequences of living in resilient ways and with resilient capabilities are profound. In reorienting itself from an emphasis on pathology to a conceptualization of adaptive functioning, ego psychology has underscored the importance of a person's capability to employ flexible coping strategies that allow one to balance change with stability, and transform circumstances rather than be transformed by them (Fine, 1990). Bandura's concept of self-efficacy also has relevancy to resilience. Self-efficacy was conceptualized by Bandura as one's ability to feel competent to live life effectively and be able to readily cope with life's struggles (Bandura, 1997). Flach's Law of Disruption and Reintegration insinuates that psychological distress and the feeling of "falling apart" are necessary for personal growth. He explains that in an episode in which one feels utterly defeated, in which it seems there is nothing to gain, a unique opportunity arises: the potential to elucidate past suffering, learn new ways to overcome struggles, and reconceptualize one's life perspective. One who is resilient recognizes the value of these opportunities and uses them effectively not simply to surmount adversity, but to surpass their previous echelon of capabilities (Richardson, Neiger, Jensen, & Kumpfer, 1990).

Resilient individuals seem to embody several common characteristics and abilities. In her doctoral dissertation, *Resiliency among lesbians and bisexual women during the process of self-acceptance and disclosure of their sexual orientation*, Colleen Gregory (1998) lists eight substantiated factors defining resilience: problem-solving abilities (perceive problems as naturally occurring), ability to recruit social support (creating reciprocal and meaningful support systems), a driving will to overcome (a constant investment in the self, determination to not be broken, and constant fight to triumph over adversity), persistent hope (the construction of positive perceptions of adversity and consistent focus on a positive future), achievement orientation (an eagerness to learn and succeed, curiousness and goal-directed), sense of purpose (commitment to some service or venture to make meaning of experiences), belief in Higher Force (a spiritual awareness that acts as support when other kinds are absent), and a sense of humor (a protective factor that "offers momentary relief, enriches interpersonal relationships, facilitates discussion of a painful subject, and provides a sense of control, even when there is none") (Gregory, 1998, p. 17).

The Case Against Gay and Lesbian Parenting

Adversaries of lesbian and gay parental rights claim that children with lesbian or gay parents will fall victim to several negative outcomes. As Rekers and Kilgus (2001) discuss, the most common concerns related to gay and lesbian parenting are the future orientation of the child, early sexual experiences, gender identity, understanding of sex roles, and other risks that may lead to social or psychological quandaries. Probably the most prevalent is the concern of children, themselves, becoming gay or lesbian. This is in part a result of a prominent study conducted in England by London researchers Golombok and Tasker (1996) in which they state that children of gays and lesbians are more likely to experiment with same-sex sexual behavior as a consequence of the more accepting climate created in the family by gay and lesbian parents. This assertion about a more accepting climate, of course, rests on the premise that exploration of one's sexuality and an accepting environment are a disadvantage.

However, Cameron and Cameron (1996) also echo this concern as they assert that the issue is threefold encompassing the threat of homosexual tendencies in children, childhood sexual victimization by partners or acquaintances, and the likelihood of children becoming socially and psychologically disturbed by way of modeling after their "disturbed" gay or lesbian parents. The concerns usually come in three themes: sexual identity and homosexual contagion, personal development and psychological health, and social relationships. There are those who feel that children who experience the gay or lesbian lifestyle will become vulnerable to mental breakdown, maladjustment, behavioral tribulations, and psychological conflict (Cameron & Cameron, 1996). Many assertions about the lack of values embraced by gays and lesbians are based on stereotypes and misconceptions about the "homosexual lifestyle" that is considered to be indicative of promiscuity leading to an unstable environment and psuedo-monogamous relationships. Critics assume that this kind of lifestyle is typical of every gay male or lesbian. Consequently, they also assume that gays and lesbians model poor ideals about marriage as transitory and mostly for sexual pleasure. In addition, violence in the same promiscuous relationships, substance abuse, suicide risk, reduced life span, sexual identity confusion and family incest are also attributed to gays and lesbians, thus, clearly depicting a skewed public picture of same-sex parenting which is not compatible with traditional parenting ideals.

Some theorists believe that children will have difficulty in social relationships; experience stigmatization, teasing, or other forms of traumatizing by peers. Advocates against homosexual parenting fear that children simply will not have an adequate mix of gender role models. Harris and Turner (1985) surveyed a small, non-random sample of 23 gay and lesbian parents and 16 single heterosexual parents, and found that heterosexual parents made more efforts to provide an opposite-sex role model for their children. Finally, there is concern about pedophilia among gay men, a misconception (Patterson, 1992) that deeply alarms many researchers (Cameron & Cameron, 1996; Golombok, 1983; Golombok & Tasker, 1996; Koepke, 1992; Rekers & Kilgus, 1995; Turner, 1990).

Those against gay and lesbian parenting often use the nature of the subject as evidence against the significance of findings. As duly noted by researchers, methodology in this field is challenging. Koepke (1992), in her study on relationship quality in lesbian couples with and without children, echoes this, commenting on the methodological problems evident when conducting research with gays and lesbians. Similarly, Turner (1990) and colleagues take note of a bias towards white, middleclass samples that are often small in number and seldom attained by the employment of rigorous research procedures. Critics also make the point that the studies that focus on children–who had been parented by a heterosexual couple during their formative years–can be misleading (Rekers & Kilgus, 1995).

In summary, societal values about who should and is capable of parenting are heterosexist and revolve around heterosexual ideals and crass misconceptions about gays and lesbians in general. Those who uphold the idea that gays and lesbians cannot possibly raise children in a manner consistent with the values of society have failed to recognize the heterosexism both overt and covertly embedded in those values. The general perception among critics of gay and lesbian parents incorporates fears about a change from the "natural" ways to parenthood. Also entrenched in dominant culture is a driving force toward procreation as a means that this society may survive. Thus, same-sex couples are in direct conflict with this socially contracted definition of a parent, a couple, and a relationship.

The Case for Gay and Lesbian Parenting

Despite these concerns, however, most psychological research conducted thus far concludes that there is no difference in developmental outcomes between children raised by gay and lesbian parents and those raised by heterosexual parents. In response to the opposing side's stance on the validity of the research, the same methodological challenges arise in any attempted studies concerning sensitive or controversial issues. In addition, as Charlotte Patterson (1994) reflects, researchers cannot possibly determine the degree to which a sample represents a population because nobody knows the actual composition of the entire population of lesbian mothers, gay fathers, or their children. Since many of these families and individuals choose to remain in hiding, to evaluate how much a sample does or does not represent the population is meaningless. Validity will come through the combined efforts of many studies, not a single experiment as in chemistry or biology (Patterson, 1995). In their survey of 23 gay or lesbian parents, Harris and Turner (1986) concluded that effective parenting is not significantly affected by the parent's sexual orientation and, further, does not represent a major issue in the child-parent relationship. Lott-Whitehead and Tully (1992) also found that same-sex couples as well as single gay and lesbian parents are just as capable as their heterosexual counterparts to engage in successful family life. As mentioned before, the three areas of concern are gender identity (a person's self-identification as a male or female), gender-role behavior (the degree to which one's activities, occupation, etc., follow the culturally prescribed standards for masculinity or femininity), and sexual orientation (one's preference in sexual partners).

Gender Identity

Normal development of gender identity has been found among children of lesbian mothers (Kirkpatrick, Smith, & Roy, 1981). Green (1978), in an attempt to assess gender identity in lesbian and transsexual raised children, chose 21 lesbian raised and 16 transsexual raised children (aged 3-20) as subjects. All participants, except one, indicated normal gender toy, game, and clothing preference. Thirteen older subjects indicated erotic fantasies or sexual behaviors; these subjects were all heterosexual in orientation. Furthermore, Green found in another study (1986) of 56 children born to lesbian mothers and 48 children born to heterosexual mothers no difference between the groups in IQ, self-concept or social adjustment and no evidence of conflict in gender identity. Golombok, Spencer, and Rutter (1983) addressed this issue more specifically and found children to be happy with their gender.

Gender-Role Behavior

Several studies have found that gender-role behavior of children of lesbian mothers was within the normal range of traditional sex roles. No difference between children of heterosexuals and homosexuals was found in toy preference, activities, interests or career choices (Gottman, 1991; Green, 1978; Kirkpatrick et al., 1981; Patterson, 1994). Hoeffer (1981) assessed gender-role behavior among 40, 6-9 year-old children of 20 lesbian and 20 heterosexual mothers and found no significant differences between the groups in toy preferences.

Sexual Orientation

In a study of 55 gay or bisexual men with a total of 82 sons at least 17 years old, Bailey (1995) and colleagues found that among the sons over 90% of those whose orientation could be determined were heterosexual. The authors conclude that a parent's sexual orientation has no bearing on their child's sexual orientation. Huggins (1989) also found this same outcome when she interviewed 36 teenage daughters, half of whom were born to lesbian women and the other half born to heterosexual women; and no children of lesbian mothers identified as lesbian, but one child of a heterosexual mother did. Several researchers (Bailey, Bobrow, Wolfe, & Mikach, 1995; Golombok et al., 1983; Green, 1978; Huggins, 1989) have all found that the majority of children raised by gay or lesbian parent(s) in all studies describe themselves as having a heterosexual orientation (Patterson, 1995).

Personal Development

Other concerns related to personal development such as separation-individuation, psychiatric evaluations, assessments of behavior problems, personality, self-concept, locus of control, moral judgment, and intelligence in children of gay and lesbian parents have no empirical foundation among children of lesbian mothers (Patterson, 1992). Those children of gays and lesbians who were conceived through previous marriages and showed emotional tribulations were thought to have them due to the divorce between parents rather than the sexual orientation of the parents (Green, 1982). In her comparative study of adolescents with divorced lesbian and heterosexual mothers, Huggins (1989) did not find any statistically significant differences in self-esteem scores and concluded that adolescent self-esteem is not negatively influenced by a lesbian household home environment.

Social Relationships

The quality of the social relationships of children of gay and lesbian homes was found to be positive and normal in terms of same-sex best friends and peer-groups. Children of divorced lesbians were found to have more contact with their fathers than their counterparts, divorced heterosexual mothers. In a study comparing lesbian mothers with heterosexual single mothers, Green found that children raised by these mothers did not differ regarding popularity or social adjustment (Green, 1986). Golombok (1983) compared 37 children (aged 5-17 years) of lesbian households with 38 children (aged 5-17 years) of single-parent heterosexual households. Through standardized interviews and questionnaires, Golombok found no difference between the groups in gender-identity, friendships, or peer relationships; however, she did observe "proportionally higher" psychiatric problems in the heterosexual single-parent group.

Pedophilia

Pedophilia is an adult sexual attraction to children who are prepubescent. It is considered by all psychologists to be pathology (i.e., aberrant behavior). Sexual orientation (whether homosexual or heterosexual) is an adult sexual attraction to other adults. No connection between pedophilia and homosexuality has ever been found. In addition, 90% of all sexual abuse is perpetrated by heterosexual males (Jenny, 1994; Newton, 1978).

Home Environments

This literature review found no studies in which children of gay or lesbian homes were disadvantaged in any significant respect relative to children of heterosexual parents (Falk, 1994; Lott-Whitehead, 1992). Miller et al. (1981) evaluated the home-environment of 34 lesbians with 43 children and that of 47 heterosexual women with children and found that lesbian mothers were more child-oriented in certain caregiver situations. Patterson's (1994a) study revealed a significant difference among the participants: children of lesbian mothers reported greater symptoms of stress, but also a greater overall sense of well-being in comparison to children from the heterosexual family group.

Opposite-Sex Role Models

Children come into contact with opposite-sex role models in virtually every aspect of their life. There are plenty of opportunities for children to gain the valuable relationships with opposite-sex adult role models through school, activities, family, and extended family and friends (Kirkpatrick, 1987).

Literature Review Summary

It seems the research confirms that sexual orientation does not significantly influence one's ability to parent well and that lesbianism itself does not negatively influence the development of children. The sexual orientation of a parent has not been shown to affect the sexual orientation of her/his child, and children of gays and lesbians are no more likely to be gay than any other child. Actually, lesbian homes were found to provide a more nurturing and accepting environment (Lott-Whitehead & Tully, 1992). The APA has concluded that "home environments provided by gay and lesbian parents are as likely as those provided by heterosexual parents to support and enable children's psychosocial growth" (APA, 2004, resolution section, ¶ 6). Some evidence says that children of gays and lesbians are more tolerant of diversity, but this is in no way a disadvantage. Some children of gay and lesbian homes will grow up to be gay, as will children of heterosexual homes. Those raised by gays and lesbians will have the added advantage of being raised by supportive and accepting parents.

The purpose of this research was to explore the process by which lesbians become parents, explore the details of lesbian family life, and evaluate the mechanisms by which these lesbian families have learned to survive. In addition, this research contributes to the depth of the existing research as well as supporting previous conclusions drawn by other researchers. Further, this qualitative study reflects upon the strength, compassion, and insight found among the women forging these new patterns of family dynamics and societal reconfigurations. The implications of such family structure and participants' struggles were examined with particular emphasis given to the profound resiliency exemplified by the eight families interviewed.

METHOD

Participants

The researcher interviewed eight families headed by parents who identified themselves as lesbian. Six of these were headed by lesbian couples, and two were headed by a single lesbian mother (n = 14 total participants) with a total of 17 children. Four of these families had children from previous heterosexual marriages only, two families had children through artificial insemination, one family had adopted internationally, and one family had one child through international adoption and the other two from a previous marriage. Twelve children were from previous heterosexual marriages, three children were from artificial insemination, two children were internationally adopted at six months and 9.5 months. Parents ranged in age from 36 years to 70 years, with a mean of 47 years and a median of 45.5 years. The current ages of the children ranged from six months to 45 years with a mean of 20.08 years and a median of 35 years. The age range of the 12 children from previous marriages at the time of the divorce and/or mother's coming out was one year to 30 years with a mean of 13.75 years and a median of 9.5 years. All families were of middle to upper-middle class socioeconomic status and most participants were at least college educated. Families resided in the following areas of California: Lake Tahoe (4 families), Berkeley (3 families), and Alameda (1 family).

Materials

Interviews were conducted using an original interview script (see Appendix A). This script followed a specific line of questioning about family demographic information history; current, past and ex-partners and/or ex-spouses; and legal process if applicable. The script asked interviewees to report any feelings of discrimination and reflect upon the characteristics of their children: children's peer relationships and social skills, gender identity, feelings about homosexuality, and school performance. Further, the interviewer asked about religion or spirituality, available opposite-sex role models, and positive and negative ramifications of their unique family structure, as well as their personal response to critics.

Procedure

This qualitative study involved in-depth interviews with the parents of lesbian families. Families were contacted through the following resources: PFLAG (Parents and Friends of Lesbians and Gays), COLAGE (Children of Lesbians and Gays Everywhere), Circle of Friends in the Tahoe Basin, Our Family Coalition, Families Like Ours, and AASK (Adopt A Special Kid). Through these organizations eight lesbian families volunteered to be interviewed either over the phone or over lunch. Participants were each given a disclosure explaining the purpose of the research and the qualifications of the researcher as an undergraduate student unable to give post-research counseling. Participants were required to sign waivers agreeing to these terms. During a two-month period, in-depth interviews were conducted with the adult members of each individual family. If parents consisted of a couple, both partners were interviewed together. Interviews typically lasted about one and one-half hour, although time limits were not set. Informed consent forms were completed. Constant comparative analysis (Denzin & Lincoln, 2005) was used to find patterns in the behavior and experiences of resiliency among the parents and children of the participating families. Reflexivity was a valuable component in the analysis of the interviews. This is understood as an enriched ability to see and understand resilience in the families studied because the interviewer participates in the experience that she is investigating.

RESULTS

Qualitative Research

The data collected in this study was qualitative in nature. Being a qualitative study, this research extends unique qualities that other more quantitative studies may not be able to offer. While quantitative researchers frown upon small sample sizes with concerns of generalizability, researcher involvement and convenience samples, qualitative mind frames celebrate the ability to delve deep into the intricacies of a single person's experiences regarding a specific topic. Qualitative researchers also value the efficient use of time and resources to gain refreshing perspective and new details that may be lost in the cumbersome nature of statistical undertakings. Qualitative researchers acknowledge the interest and emotional investment of a researcher and value this relationship believing that it enhances rather than skews studies. By allowing these special and non-traditional methods of study, qualitative research is often found best-suited for non-traditional research concerning issues that are thought provoking, action insinuating and newly embarked-upon (Camic, Rhodes, & Yardley, 2003; Maxwell, 1996). The aim of this study is descriptive in nature, and thus statistical analyses were not performed. All data collected is appropriately based upon self-report, respecting the expertise a participant is able to provide about her/his own personal life journey. The small sample size used in this research is not intended to speak to generalizability, nevertheless this is not to say that the public, in general, and the psychological community, at large, cannot benefit from the discussion about specific patterns concerning lesbian family resiliency put forward here. Certain patterns did emerge, some of which were unique to this study, and others which accurately confirmed previous research.

Gaining Parental Rights

Participants gained parental rights through several means. Some families had completed the process, some were amidst the legalities of this process and others were planning for the legal undertakings of gaining parental rights for their partner. Most families viewed their lack of legal rights as a disadvantage and felt like a target of discrimination in this sense. However, all families considered their unique family complete, with or without the acknowledgement of the legal system. Among all families the struggle to become parents was trying, costly, and clearly imprinted upon their family memory.

Of the two families who underwent international adoption, both chose to adopt from China. One family who had two children (14 and 21 years at the time of research) from a previous marriage adopted a six month-old (three years at the time of research) from southern China. Due to the conservative Chinese culture, the adopting mother had to pose as a single mother. The chosen partner, also the biological mother of the two children from the previous marriage, was required to sign an affidavit stating that she was not a lesbian. The adopting mother reported the process to be challenging morally, financially, and personally; and yet a fairly smooth process that took less time than she had expected. In nine months (ironically), she was able to bring home her six month-old baby girl whom she only met after the adoption process began. At the time of research, the non-adoptive partner was planning to legally adopt the then three-year-old.

The second family had a similar experience adopting from a foreign agency. However, they reported spending approximately $15,000 on adoption fees, lawyer fees and travel. This family described having to endure the adoption process twice in order for both partners to have legal rights. This family acknowledged the liberal attitudes of California and was happy to be able to adopt in that state rather than other states where the social workers conducting the home stays may not have been as open to lesbian adoption. These parents are very active in the LGBT community and have a variety of friends with internationally adopted children as well.

While the international adoption experiences seem to be the most complicated, the artificial insemination experiences were surprisingly the least complicated for this sample. For one family, the biological mother who was originally artificially inseminated was deemed unfit by the courts and moved away while the children were raised by the non-biological partner who had no legal rights to the children other than those afforded to her by the good graces of the biological mother. This participant explains the situation as scary, living off the "good will" of her ex-partner and raising teenagers as a "defacto-parent." She explains the frustration that defines her role as the sole provider, for all intent and purposes, for her children with no legal rights other than those given to her by the biological mother. She described feeling powerless, stuck and at the mercy of agencies knowing very little about her family to determine family decisions. This particular mother spoke with such strength, recognizing the almost paralyzing fear, yet owning confidence in her abilities as a provider, mother and woman. In raising her children and at the same time not being recognized as their mother, this mother was able to provide for them, care for them, make healthy decisions concerning her ex-partner and compassionately put the children before any conveniences of her own.

While this woman's story is one of hardship and obstacles, another mother who gave birth through artificial insemination described the process as "smooth" without setbacks or fears. This mother gave birth to a healthy boy with her partner of now over 13 years. For this family legalities and ex-partners were not issues. In fact, this couple described the tremendous support, extra time, energy and presence a partner can contribute in raising a child. The literature agrees that a child with parents in a committed, loving relationship is ideal. Parents with partners, regardless of sexual orientation, have an added benefit that makes the creation of a healthy home environment more readily possible compared to the struggles that single parenthood poses. Dual parent families are better equipped to handle the curve balls life can and will throw particularly in the case of these minority families. While each partner must have the same resilient characteristics of a single parent, the load is lightened by the support that is gained through a healthy, loving, and committed relationship. When parents are emotionally and psychologically more balanced, the children are as well.

Parenting Philosophy

The lesbian families interviewed exemplified compassion, strength and unconditional love for their children and their family unit. Many of the families refer to themselves as "open-minded" and "loving." A common theme which ran through all eight families was one of open communication. These lesbian families, having endured hardship, struggle, and having been able to make it work somehow—all value honesty and the ability to draw strength from one another. Mothers often explained that parenting is a true highlight in their lives; "[we] just like being in their lives . . . really like to spend time with our kids." Families all expressed encouraging their children to be independent and described the ease in which they try to respect each other's space and personal choices; especially those families whose children were teenagers. As one participant explained, "we are much more concerned about how [our children] conduct their lives rather than who they're with [romantically]" concerning parent's reactions if their children were also gay.

Another mother commented that her goal is to provide her son a "safe structure for [him] learning to reveal [him]self."

An older lesbian couple explained, "we like to nurture her imagination . . . lay a foundation for her . . . children with older parents have the advantage of just knowing more–patience, wisdom . . . we are devoted, not distracted . . . we get to share the world; I just appreciate, it's a privilege to be able to raise her."

Ramifications of Being Raised in a Homophobic Society

Several mothers commented that they see their children growing up in a healthy, stable, loving environment. Often, they described the struggles they and their children must overcome, and how these struggles create sensitivity to diversity, a sense of compassion and a realistic view of the world which only strengthens the individuality they strive to foster. Families also discussed positive ramifications of an equalitarian relationship in that equal responsibility for household chores and respect for a well-rounded individual capable of traditionally male and female tasks was modeled for the children. Appropriately, one participant stated that "the better part of parenting, whether you're straight or gay, is role modeling."

Some families discussed the hardship which not being acknowledged as a couple can create, that their relationship is not taken seriously and thus, their family suffers. One mother added that her employer does not recognize parental leave for adoptive parents. For several families, the children were split between two households especially in the case of a divorce. This was seen as especially hard on the children because they must compromise between two sets of rules, two understandings of parenting roles and two models for how a family looks and acts.

For other mothers, it was their own "coming out" story from which they draw strength and resiliency. One participant explained that her own mother wrote her out of the will upon discovering that she identified as a lesbian late in life. Worse yet, this participant's father simply wrote her out of his life. Yet, she demanded explanations and provoked open communication in order to forge new relationships with her parents as a person rather than a child. This is another example of exceptional resiliency and capability for persistence. Often, a parent's attitudes about their children's sexuality stem more from guilt that they are responsible for letting them down in some way, which triggers defensive behavior, rather than ill thoughts about the children themselves.

Psychological Well-Being and Levels of Self-Esteem

Much of the research has shown that children of lesbian parents often show high levels of general psychological well-being, and that pattern emerged in this study as well. Based on self-reports by the parents, children of this sample, in general, were described as exhibiting high levels of psychological well-being as well as high levels of self-esteem. Based on the parent reports of children, a difference did emerge for children of single lesbian households in comparison to those of lesbian couple households with higher levels of psychological well-being and self-esteem being reported by the parents of children of lesbian couples. Children seemed to fare better when their home environment was stable and their mother's partner played the role of a second parent.

Among the lesbian parents interviewed, mothers' perceptions of their own psychological health appeared to influence the extent to which they were able to be open about their lesbian sexuality with their children, friends, family, co-workers, and ex-husbands. In those cases where the ex-husband was disapproving and not supportive of the biological mother's lesbian identity, lower self-esteem was reported among children. In those cases involving a previous marriage, any disturbances among the children were thought to be linked to the divorce itself, rather than to the parents' sexual orientation.

Age of Disclosure

The age at which the child was told of his or her mother's sexual orientation emerged as a theme which helped to determine the degree of acceptance that that child was able to hold for her/his mother's sexual preference. Further, this age factor was also indicative of a child's ability to cope with social stigma and assert resilient behavior. Those children who were adopted at a young age and those whose parents "came out" during their childhood or late adolescence were more receptive than those children who were told of their mother's lesbian sexual preference during their early or middle adolescence or early adulthood. The degree to which the children were open about their parents' sexuality with their peers was related to their level of self-esteem and feelings of isolation or uniqueness from other children.

Role Models

All families in this study have established an extended family that helps to raise the child and are comprised of many opposite-sex role models from teachers to uncles and grandparents to neighbors, friends and coaches. Of those families who had children from a previous marriage, the father was involved in the children's lives despite ill feelings towards the mother, in some cases because of her sexual preference. Several mothers described this as one the greatest challenges they faced–that of remaining amiable with their ex-male partners in order to maintain an opposite-sex role model and father figure for their children. One single lesbian mother explained, "It really does take the entire village to raise a child" in describing her "extended family" who helped raise her children and serve as all different kinds of role models.

Social Skills, Gender Identity, and Emotional Stability

Children of all participants were reported by their parents to have an "adequate" sense of their gender identity. Several children at the time of study were actively seeking out confirming or disconfirming appropriate experiences as part of a natural process of identity formation exploration. The mothers believed that their children felt free to do this without fear of judgment or pressure to adhere to any ideals or fantasies. With the exception of one participant's daughter, all children were also reported to be emotionally stable given normal fluctuation. Again, emotional disturbances that did exist were seen only in the families with children from previous marriages and these disturbances were seen as a result of the divorce. In the one exception case, the daughter was reported as being exceptionally rebellious; again, this was thought by her mother to be a result of the unfriendly relationship between the parents and demeaning attitude of the father concerning his ex-wife's lesbian identity.

All mothers reported their children to have excellent social skills. In fact, several families mentioned that being "different" increased the necessity that their children adhere to social norms and learn that much more to "fit in" and pay attention to social cues. Most of the older children (high school age and older) had gay and lesbian friends and were willing to speak openly about their parent's sexual orientation as well as their own. These children were reported to feel free to explore their own sexual orientation knowing that their mothers would support their preference and desires concerning their personal life choices. Specifically, a mother described her daughter as having been involved in romantic relationships with boys and girls, but not acting particularly uncomfortable with this or in any way worried about her ultimate sexuality. This mother felt that her daughter had a healthy attitude toward sexual identity and preference and understood that these were her choices to make as she wills.

Children's Worldview

All parents felt that their children were more open and tolerant of diversity as a result of the "complexities of their own reality." Many participants denoted the ways in which their children are more non-judgmental and appreciative of diversity in the world compared to their peers. One example given by the mothers of an adopted four-year-old little girl while getting made up as a pirate for Halloween, "well if a little boy comes to school in a dress, I won't laugh."

Of course other families with adult children explained the extremely painful relationships that became non-existent when the mother "came-out" to her older children. In this way, these mothers felt that the conservative values of society have kept her children at a distance. For one older woman with children well into adulthood, emotional hardship has stemmed not necessarily from her community, but from the misunderstanding of her own children. One adult child, in particular, is very unaccepting of her lifestyle as a lesbian and this mother longs to have a close relationship with this daughter again. Yet it is through persistence and vigor that she stands in truth that is her own. "If we're not living the truth, we're living in a prison . . . oh my gosh to die and not have lived!" this resilient participant exclaims. She further advises, "be who you are and nothing less." Clearly, the emotional pains endured by these participants are examples of resilient behavior. When the power of society has overwhelmed even the closest of bonds, the resilient mother lives on and survives. For the most part, adult children expressed proud feelings that their mothers were able to be authentic and be honest with them.

DISCUSSION

This study was descriptive and, therefore, does not purport to adhere to traditional experimental design. This descriptive study also does not contend to have utilized a representative sample suitable for generalizability. Principal researcher involvement in data collection, while problematic in quantitative studies, is seen as a method of reflexivity in qualitative research in which the controversial and emotionally salient topic is better explored through the eyes of an ally struggling with the same obstacles. Lastly, as this study did rely upon self-report data, the interpretation of this must be seen in light of the researcher's own values, cultural biases and experiences which are, for the most part, similar to the participants. This dynamic allows participants and researcher to work together in revealing an intricate puzzle of the human experience which involves life, family, tradition, struggle, emotion, and may determine future policy. Qualitative research does not concern itself with inter-rater reliability; rather, the experience of each rater is valued (Camic, Rhodes, & Yardley, 2003). The sample was biased toward well-educated, upper middle-class, white individuals. There was also a regional bias in that all couples were from affluent and liberal areas of northern California.

FUTURE RESEARCH

Future research would include cross-cultural and long-term longitudinal studies which would attempt to follow children and their lesbian parents over the course of five to 10 years. Lesbian relationships have also been a neglected topic of research. Knowing more about how women relate and how lesbians, as women, negotiate their roles as both, would render valuable insight which may profoundly affect children or the perception that children are possible and wonderful additions to a family. Most importantly, there is a need for research concerning how to help the children of lesbians cope with the struggle society presents them with on a daily basis. Lesbians often report that first they are women and second they are lesbian. One's sexual preference is only a small part of the whole that we as humans are capable of being. It is no surprise, then, that the women of this study are strong, brave, loving, nurturing, sensitive, and unrelenting.

In summary, it seems that the fears of a resistant culture have hampered the full acceptance of gays and lesbians as parents. However, past research confirms that gay and lesbian parents are just as fit for the job as heterosexual parents. The data collected in this study confirms previous findings that demonstrated that the home environment provided by lesbian couples is no less capable of being beneficial to children, and may prove to be more stable, healthy, and accepting than environments provided by some single, heterosexual parents.

Parenting ability is determined by the will, devotion, love and the ability to provide for and nurture a child; sexual orientation is irrelevant to a child's mental health. The fact that gays and lesbians become parents as a result of thoughtful planning and fervent desire to love a child and give that child their wisdom and knowledge shows a devotion to parenting that most children will not have the luxury of experiencing in caretakers. Often these non-traditional families exemplify and maintain the values and roles of traditional families including support, loyalty, love, values, welfare and affection. As one subject said, "the success rate of straight families isn't so profound that people should be throwing stones."

New York Surrogate Court Judge, Eve Preminger, summarized the issue best when ruling in favor of the second-parent adoption of Evan, 583 N.Y.S.2d 997, 1002 in 1992.

> This is not a matter which arises in a vacuum. Social fragmentation and the myriad configurations of modern families have presented us with new problems and complexities that cannot be solved by idealizing the past. Today a child who receives proper nutrition, adequate schooling and supportive sustaining shelter is among the fortunate, whatever the source. A child who also receives the love and nurture of even a single parent can be counted among the blessed. Here this court finds a child who has all the above benefits and two adults dedicated to his welfare, secure in their loving partnership and determined to raise him to the very best of their considerable abilities. There is no reason in law, logic or social philosophy to obstruct such a favorable situation. (Newman, 2005, p. 558)

The research has shown time and time again that lesbian parenting causes no harm to children, but rather it is limitations that society places upon these parents that force their children to contend with the burdens of vicarious social stigma. The concern for parental sexual orientation stems from a political need to keep change under control. It is of no consequence to the raising of a child and thus the efforts and struggles of gay and lesbian parents should be celebrated and commended, rather than discouraged, disregarded or sabotaged.

NOTE

1. Census 2000 counts underestimate the actual gay, lesbian, and bisexual population of the United States by not including single gay males and single lesbians (Census questions did not ask about sexual orientation, behavior or attraction). Same-sex couples were determined as such if the household member filling out the Census form

identified an adult of his or her same-sex as the "husband/wife" or "unmarried partner." Thus, this may represent an undercount as for reasons of confidentiality, some same-sex couples may choose to remain unidentified to government and/or may define their relationship in terms of something other than "husband/wife" or "unmarried partner." Badgett and Rodgers contend that the Census Bureau missed at least 16 to 19 percent of the total gay and lesbian coupled population. Further, "if 5 percent of the U.S. adult population is gay or lesbian and approximately 30 percent of gay men and lesbians are coupled (as several surveys suggest), then Census figures did not count 62 percent of all same-sex couples" (Bennett & Gates, 2003, p. 7).

REFERENCES

American Psychological Association (2004, July 28 & 30). Policy Statement: Sexual Orientation, Parents & Children. Retrieved January 27, 2006 from the World Wide Web: http://www.apa.org/pi/lgbc/policy/parents.html
Bailey, J., Bobrow, D., Wolfe, M., & Mikach, S. (1995). Sexual orientation of adult sons of gay fathers. _Developmental Psychology, 31,_ 124-129.
Bandura, A. (1997). _Self Efficacy: The exercise of control._ New York: W.H. Freeman and Co.
Bennett, L., & Gates, G. (2003). The Cost of Marriage Inequality to Children and their Same-Sex Parents: A Human Rights Campaign Foundation Report. Retrieved January 27, 2006, from the World Wide Web: http://www.hrc.org/familynet
Bigner, J. (2000). Gay and lesbian families. In W. C. Nichols, M. A. Pace-Nichols, D. S. Becvar, & A. Y. Napier (Eds.), _Handbook of family development and intervention_ (pp. 279-298). Hoboken, NJ: John Wiley & Sons.
Cameron, P., & Cameron, K. (1996). Homosexual parents. _Adolescence, 31,_ 757-768.
Camic, P., Rhodes, J., & Yardley, L. (2003). _Qualitative research in psychology: Expanding perspectives in methodology and design._ Washington, DC: American Psychological Association.
Cost of Adopting. National Adoption Information Clearinghouse (2000). Retrieved October 6, 2002 from the World Wide Web: www.calib.com/naic/pubs/s_cost.htm.
Denzin, N., & Lincoln, Y. (2005). _Sage handbook of qualitative research (3rd Ed.)._ Thousand Oaks, CA: Sage.
Executive Summary of Adoption Laws (2002). Adoption Family Center (AFC), Families Like Ours, Inc. Retrieved July 26, 2002 from the World Wide Web: http://www.adoptionfamilycenter.org/resources/states/bythenumbers.htm
Falk, P. (1994). The gap between psychosocial assumptions and empirical research in lesbian mother child custody cases. In A. E. Gottfried & A. W. Gottfried (Eds.), _Redefining families: Implications for children's development_ (pp. 131-156). New York: Plenum.
Fine, S. (1990). Resilience and human adaptability: Who rises above adversity? _American Journal of Occupational Therapy, 45,_ 493-503.
Flaks, D., Ficher, I., Masterpasqua, F., & Joseph, G. (1995). Lesbians choosing motherhood. A comparative study of lesbian and heterosexual parents and their children. _Developmental Psychology, 31,_ 105-114.

Golombok, S., Spencer, A., & Rutter, M. (1983). Children in lesbian and single-parent households: Psychosexual and psychiatric appraisal. *Journal of Child Psychology & Psychiatry, 24,* 551-572.

Golombok, S., & Tasker, F. (1996). Do parents influence the sexual orientation of their children? Findings from a longitudinal study of lesbian families. *Developmental Psychology, 32*(3), 3-11.

Green, R. (1978). Sexual identity of 37 children raised by homosexual or transsexual parents. *American Journal of Psychiatry, 135,* 692-697.

Green, R., Mandel, J., Hotvedt, M., Gray, J., & Smith, L. (1986). Lesbian mothers and their children: A comparison with solo parent heterosexual mothers and their children. *Archives of Sexual Behavior, 15,* 167-184.

Green, R. (1982). The best interest of the child with a lesbian mother. *Bulletin of the American Academy of Psychiatry and the Law, 10,* 7-15.

Gregory, C. (1998). *Resiliency among lesbians and bisexual women during the process of self-acceptance and disclosure of their sexual orientation.* Unpublished doctoral dissertation, University of Rhode Island, Kingston.

Harris, M., & Turner, P. (1986). Gay and lesbian parents. *Journal of Homosexuality, 12,* 101-112.

Hoeffer, B. (1981). Children's acquisitions of sex-role behavior in lesbian-mother families. *American Journal of Orthopsychiatry, 51,* 536-544.

Hollinger, J. (2000). *Adoption law and practice.* New York: Matthew Bender & Company.

HRC Family Net. Human Rights Council. Retrieved January 15th, 2006 from the World Wide Web: http://www.hrc.org/familynet

HRC Marriage Center. Human Rights Council. Retrieved January 15th, 2006 from the World Wide Web: http://www.hrc.org/marriage

Huggins, S. (1989). A comparative study of self-esteem of adolescent children of divorced lesbian mothers and divorced heterosexual mothers. *Journal of Homosexuality, 18 (1/2),* 123-135.

Jenny, C., Roesler, T. A. & Poyer, K. L. (1994). Are children at risk for sexual abuse by homosexuals? *Pediatrics, 94*(1), 41-44.

Kirk, J. (2005). Gay Adoptions: Defining Triumph Against Adversity. Retrieved October 23, 2005 from the World Wide Web: http://www. proudparenting.com

Kirkpatrick, M., Smith, C., & Roy, R. (1981). Lesbian mothers and their children: A comparative survey. *American Journal of Orthopsychiatry, 51,* 545-551.

Kirkpatrick, M. (1987). Clinical implications of lesbian mother studies. *Journal of Homosexuality, 14* (1 & 2), 201-211.

Koepke, L., Hare, J., & Moran, P. (1992). Relationship quality in a sample of lesbian couples with children and child-free lesbian couples. *Family Relations, 41,* 224, 225.

Lott-Whitehead, L., & Tully, C. (1992). The family of lesbian mothers. *Smith College Studies in Social Work, 63,* 265-280.

Martin, A. (1993). *The lesbian and gay parenting handbook.* New York: Harper-Collins.

Maxwell, J. A. (1996). *Qualitative Research Design: An interactive approach* (Vol. 41). Thousand Oaks, CA: Sage.

Miller, J., Jacobsen, R., & Bigner, J. J. (1981). The child's home environment for lesbian vs. heterosexual mothers: A neglected area of research. *Journal of Homosexuality, 7,* 49-56.

Nelson, F. (1999). Lesbian families: Achieving motherhood. *Journal of Gay & Lesbian Social Services,10*(1), 27-46.

Nelson, F. (1996). *Lesbian motherhood: An exploration of Canadian lesbian families.* Toronto: University of Toronto Press.

Newman, S. A. (2005). The use and abuse of social science in the same-sex marriage debate. *New York Law School Law Review, 49,* 537-561.

Newton, D. (1978). Homosexual behavior and child molestation: A review of the evidence. *Adolescence, 8*(49), 40.

Patterson, C. (1992). Children of lesbian and gay parents. *Child Development, 63,* 1025-1042.

Patterson, C. (1994). Children of the lesbian baby boom: Behavioral adjustment, self-concepts, and sex-role identity. In B. Green & G. Herek (Eds.), *Contemporary perspectives of gay and lesbian psychology: Theory, research, and applications* (pp. 156-175). Beverly Hills, CA: Sage.

Patterson, C. (1994a). Lesbian and gay couples considering parenthood: An agenda for research, service, and advocacy. *Journal of Gay & Lesbian Social Services, 1*(2), 33-55.

Patterson, C. (1995). Lesbian mothers, gay fathers and their children. In A.R. D'Augelli & C. Patterson (Eds.), *Lesbian, gay and bisexual identities across the lifespan: Psychological perspectives* (pp. 262-290). New York: Oxford University.

Patterson, C. (2004). Lesbian and gay parents and their children: Summary of research findings. In *Lesbian and gay parenting: A resource for psychologists* (pp. 1 - 12). Washington, DC: American Psychological Association.

Patterson, C., Fulcher, M., & Wainright, J. (2002). Children of lesbian and gay parents: Research, law, and policy. In B. L. Bottoms, M. B. Kovera, & B. D. McAuliff (Eds.), *Children, Social science and the law* (pp. 176-199). New York: Cambridge University Press.

Pennington, S. (1987). Children of lesbian mothers. In F. W. Bozett (Ed.), *Gay and lesbian parents* (pp. 58-174). New York: Praeger.

Rekers, G., & Kilgus, M. (1995). Studies of homosexual parenting: A critical review. *Regent University Law Review, 14,* 343-384.

Richardson, G., Neiger, B., Jensen, S., & Kumpfer, K. (1990). The resiliency model. *Health Education,* Nov-Dec, 33-37.

Sexual orientation and the law (1990). *Harvard law review.* Cambridge: Harvard University.

Siegenthaler, A. L., & Bigner, J. J. (2000). The value of children to lesbian and non-lesbian mothers. *Journal of Homosexuality, 39*(2), 73-91.

Slater, S. (1995). *The lesbian family life cycle.* New York: Free Press.

Sullivan, A. (1995). Policy issues in gay and lesbian adoption. *Adoption and Fostering, 19*(4), 21-25.

Sullivan, A. (1996). Let gays marry. *Newsweek,* June 27, 26-28.

Turner, P., Scadden, L., & Harris, M. B. (1990). Parenting in gay and lesbian families. *Journal of Gay & Lesbian Psychotherapy, 1,* 55-56.

Wahler, R., & Smith, G. (1999). Effective parenting as the integration of lessons and dialogue. *Journal of Child & Family Studies, 8*(2), 135-149.

doi:10.1300/J086v18n01_02

APPENDIX A
INTERVIEW SCRIPT QUESTIONS:

Is _____ Biological, Adopted, Previous Heterosexual Marriage or conceived otherwise?
Contact with Mother/ Father?
Do you both have parental rights?

Adoption Type:
Was the process challenging?
Obstacles?
Discrimination?
What is the role of your (ex-spouse, past partner, current partner) in your child(ren)'s life(s)?
What is your involvement with the GLB community?
Religion?
Parenting Philosophy?
Child(ren)'s feelings about homosexuality?
Child(ren)'s feelings about your involvement in the GLB community?
Describe their friends?
Describe their role at school?
    Play behavior?
    Gender Identity?
    Social Skills?
    Performance?
Do they like school?
Puberty?
Opposite Sex Role Models?
What if _____grew up gay?
Negative Ramifications?
    Plans to Nullify?
Positive Ramifications?
    Response to Critics?

Application of Feminist Therapy: Promoting Resiliency Among Lesbian and Gay Families

Charles Negy
Cliff McKinney

SUMMARY. Lesbian and gay (LG) parents face common and unique challenges compared to heterosexual parents. In addition to the typical challenges that all parents encounter while rearing children, LG parents often face myriad obstacles to having and rearing children in a society that struggles to accept alternative family structures. In this paper, we provide a brief overview of the empirical literature related to LG parenting and children of same-sex couples. Then, some fundamental principles of feminist theory as they relate to the provision of therapy are discussed. Last, we present a case study that exemplifies judicious application of feminist therapy as a means to validate, strengthen, and promote resiliency among the family members of a lesbian couple who had sought treatment. Future directions of research with LG families are discussed. doi:10.1300/J086v18n01_03 *[Article copies available for a fee from The Haworth Document Delivery Service: 1-800-HAWORTH. E-mail address: <docdelivery@haworthpress.com> Website: <http://www.HaworthPress.com> © 2006 by The Haworth Press, Inc. All rights reserved.]*

KEYWORDS. Lesbian and gay, parenting, feminist therapy, resiliency

[Haworth co-indexing entry note]: "Application of Feminist Therapy: Promoting Resiliency Among Lesbian and Gay Families." Negy, Charles, and Cliff McKinney. Co-published simultaneously in *Journal of Feminist Family Therapy* (The Haworth Press, Inc.) Vol. 18, No. 1/2, 2006, pp. 67-83; and: *Lesbian Families' Challenges and Means of Resiliency: Implications for Feminist Family Therapy* (ed: Anne M. Prouty Lyness) The Haworth Press, Inc., 2006, pp. 67-83. Single or multiple copies of this article are available for a fee from The Haworth Document Delivery Service [1-800-HAWORTH, 9:00 a.m. - 5:00 p.m. (EST). E-mail address: docdelivery@haworthpress.com].

Available online at http://jfft.haworthpress.com
© 2006 by The Haworth Press, Inc. All rights reserved.
doi:10.1300/J086v18n01_03

INTRODUCTION

Controversy abounds regarding the relationships and family lives of lesbian and gay (LG) individuals (Lambert, 2005; Tasker, 2005). Perhaps owing to a heterosexist view, LG parenting has been viewed as detrimental to children. In fact, courts have consistently ruled against LG parental rights based on the idea that the stigma attached to homosexuality would cause children to be teased and ostracized, leading to psychological and social dysfunction, that children may not develop gender-appropriate feminine or masculine characteristics, or that children would grow up with an increased likelihood of being gay or lesbian (Fredriksen-Goldsen & Erera, 2003; Golombok et al., 2003; Hequembourg, 2004; Lambert, 2005; Litovich & Langhout, 2004; MacCallum & Golombok, 2004). Some of the research conducted in this area has adopted a deficit-comparison model to support (and in some instances, to deny) heterosexist claims, failing to examine the full context and even possible advantages of LG parenting (Tasker, 2005).

The fact that societal stereotypes continue to remain strong in the face of empirical evidence is unsettling. Not only do these stereotypes infringe upon the basic rights of LG individuals, they also make it difficult to conduct research regarding LG individuals and families. Accurate statistics regarding the numbers of LG families in the United States are difficult to determine due to fear of discrimination, rejection, and legal implications (Lambert, 2005; Oswald, 2002; Tasker, 2005). Because of these fears, many LG parents likely remain guarded with respect to disclosing their sexual orientation to others. Although accurate information is impossible to obtain, it has been estimated that between 2 and 14 million children are living with LG parents in the United States, and this appears to be an increasing trend (Lambert, 2005; Litovich & Langhout, 2004; Tasker, 2005).

In what follows, we first provide a brief overview of the empirical literature related to LG parenting and children of same-sex couples. Then, some fundamental principles of feminist theory as related to the provision of therapy are discussed. Last, we present a case study that exemplifies utilizing judicious application of feminist therapy as a means to validate, strengthen, and promote resiliency among the family members of a lesbian couple who had sought treatment.

CONTRASTING LG WITH HETEROSEXUAL PARENTING

Given this increasingly important aspect of society, many researchers have investigated differences between LG parents and their heterosexual counterparts. Contrary to early views that LG parents would be unfit for parenthood, some research demonstrates the opposite effect. For example, LG parents typically adopt a child-centered approach to rearing their children and LG partners generally are highly committed to maintaining family integrity (Clunis & Green, 1995; Lynch, 2000). Gay fathers, when compared to heterosexual fathers, report being firmer in setting appropriate standards for their children and employing more reasoning strategies when responding to the needs of their children (Tasker, 2005). Further, gay fathers, relative to heterosexual fathers, do not differ in their intimacy or involvement with their children and show higher levels of warmth and responsiveness combined with control and limit-setting in their parenting patterns (Lambert, 2005).

Research demonstrates that lesbian mothers generally stress to their children factors such as tolerance for diversity (Eldridge & Barrett, 2003; Lambert, 2005) and that they are more aware of the necessary skills for effective parenting than heterosexual parents (Vanfraussen, Ponjaert-Kristoffersen, & Brewaeys, 2003). Lesbian mothers, relative to heterosexual mothers, often prove to be superior in their ability to discover critical issues in child-care situations and to effect appropriate solutions. Lesbian mothers also tend to express greater warmth, spend more time interacting with their children, and have interactions with their children that are higher in quality (Vanfraussen et al., 2003).

Although some research demonstrates positive characteristics of LG parents, no known research that we could find has found that LG parents, on average, manifest more negative qualities than heterosexual parents. Given the fact that LG parents often face unique challenges that heterosexual parents do not, such as discrimination in myriad contexts (Fredriksen-Goldsen & Erera, 2003; Hequembourg, 2004), researchers have speculated about possible factors that may contribute to the resiliency of LG parenting.

Resiliency in LG Parents

Resilience research concentrates on relational processes that assist family survival and growth under unfavorable circumstances (Oswald, 2002). That body of literature, by and large, has focused on non-sexual minority individuals, such as adolescents or racial minorities. Consequently, the applicability of those findings to LG parents and their children is less than certain (Litovich & Langhout, 2004).

LG families must be flexible in order to establish and maintain a family in the contemporary United States (Halstead, 2003; Lynch, 2000). Commitment between same-sex partners is largely unrecognized by the legal system and, as such, LG couples experience a lack of legal support and parental rights (Krestan & Bepko, 1980; Oswald, 2002). Further, newly forming LG families must adjust to new roles. For example, LG parents must decide if both individuals will act as equal partners in parenting or if one of them will be viewed as a big brother/sister or as a close family member (Tasker, 2005). A challenge faced by many LG families is that there is no schema prescribed by society as there is for heterosexual families, such as institutionalized structures approving of their status as a family (Hequembourg, 2005; Lynch, 2000). As such, LG individuals face adversity and potential discrimination when attempting to form families (Lynch, 2000).

To meet these challenges, many LG families have created ways of being a family and exhibit a unique strength and flexibility that assists all the members of their family in the transitions to family life (Lynch, 2000; Oswald, 2002). Such resiliency strategies may include intentionality and redefinition (Oswald). Intentionality includes behavioral strategies that sustain and legitimize relationships through the conscious formation, ritualization, and legalization of relationships considered as family. Further, external supports are created and the visibility of homosexuality inside and outside of their familial network is recognized and managed. Redefinition comprises semantic strategies that create symbolic and linguistic mechanisms to affirm gay and lesbian familial networks. These strategies may include the development of an inclusive and politicized view of the family, the use of familial names to reinforce relational ties (e.g., referring to friends as brother or sister), and incorporation of homosexuality with significant life dimensions (e.g., emphasizing the importance of identity in various aspects of life [Oswald, 2002]).

Further research has demonstrated that, in response to oppression, lesbian individuals develop a strong sense of self, flexibility, and inclusiveness within the family and maintain equity in their relationships when they become parents, leading to increased satisfaction in both parents and children (Fredriksen-Goldsen & Erera, 2003; Hequembourg, 2004). LG families often cope with oppression by developing mutual, balanced, and interdependent family relationships (Connolly, 2005). In light of the lack of negative differences between LG and heterosexual parents and the empirically observed positive qualities in LG parents, some researchers have investigated LG parenting effects on children.

Children of Same-Sex Couples

Research suggests that children of LG parents are comparable to children of heterosexual parents, overall, on psychosocial adjustment and development and share similar experiences of family life as children of heterosexual parents (Tasker, 2005). Specifically, children are comparable with regard to gender development, personal development, social relationships, and even on sexual orientation (Lambert, 2005; Tasker, 2005). It deserves highlighting here that the majority of adolescents and young adults who have been reared by LG parents report being heterosexuals. In sum, the research on psychosocial adjustment demonstrates very few differences between children of LG versus heterosexual parents.

Research examining differences in children reared without fathers (i.e., single heterosexual parents and single or coupled lesbian parents) demonstrates that children in fatherless families experience more interaction with their mother and perceive her as more dependable and available than children from homes with fathers (MacCallum & Golombok, 2004). The only difference noted in the development of children was that boys in father-absent families demonstrated more feminine but no less masculine characteristics (MacCallum & Golombok, 2004). Research has done well to address the early concerns of courts and society. With regard to child adjustment, there is no empirical evidence that LG parenting is detrimental to development, particularly with regard to behavioral problems, peer relations, self-esteem, gender development, and sexual orientation (Golombok et al., 2003; Lambert, 2005; Litovich & Langhout, 2004; MacCallum & Golombok, 2004; Tasker, 2005). Further, children who do experience stigmatization based on the sexual orientation of their parents experience this conflict in a similar fashion as other children do who suffer from religious, ethnic, or economic oppression (Litovich & Langhout, 2004).

Instead of focusing on negative outcomes of children with LG parents, researchers need to consider possible strengths these children may display (Lambert, 2005). These strengths may include a greater appreciation of diversity, a willingness to challenge traditional sex-role stereotypes, and an ability to fashion creative, nurturing, healthy family relationships in the face of a sometimes oppressive society (Lambert, 2005).

FEMINIST THEORY AND THERAPY

In the United States, feminist therapy emerged in the 1970s, coinciding with the women's liberation movement (Avis, 1987; Hare-Mustin, 1978). Grounded in the ideas of feminist theory, feminist therapy reflects an adherence to the notion of equality and that ". . . the personal is political" (Park, 2004, p. 289). Broverman, Broverman, and Clarkson (1970) were among the first researchers to highlight, based on their study, how mainstream therapists often failed to consider sociocultural variables, such as rigid sex-role demands, cultural expectations, and discrimination in the etiology of women's psychological problems. Feminist therapy is eclectic in the sense that it utilizes techniques from other approaches to therapy. However, it is value-driven, rather than being technically driven (Hill & Ballou, 1998). According to Park, feminist therapy "should not be viewed as a set of therapeutic techniques, but instead as 'a sensibility' " (p. 290).

Some of the elements of contemporary therapy driven by a feminist sensibility include the following:

a. Respect for women and their experiences. Therapists can provide a vital function to female clients by acknowledging and validating women's reality as they subjectively experience the world. This includes acknowledging that the world, for many women, is one in which they are judged in accordance with standards established by men (McGoldrick, Anderson, & Walsh, 1989; Prouty, 2001).

b. Attentiveness to language. According to Park (2004), applying a feminist sensibility to the context of therapy includes focusing on the ways in which language both expresses and constructs clients' experiences. An attentive therapist will tend to the layers of meaning that may be inherent in a woman's narrative–a narrative that may not be readily understood against the norms of masculine discourse. For example, a client who is dissatisfied with her weight may be, in actuality, manifesting her internalization of patriarchal and unrealistic ideals of female beauty.

c. Sociocultural variables as the etiology of psychopathology. In general, instead of assuming a woman's distress is the result of intrapsychic dysfunction, feminist therapists will consider the likelihood that the distress is symptomatic of pathological cultural norms (Walters, Carter, Papp, & Silverstein, 1988). Such norms may include oppression in the form of social attitudes that promulgate female inferiority or even contempt of women (i.e., misogyny) and behavioral discrimination, such as workplace discrimination, inadequate child care, and so on.

d. Commitment to social change. Understanding the pernicious consequences of oppression, therapists may want to go beyond the therapy setting and seek public and professional avenues through which they may vocalize their condemnation of existing power structures and societal attitudes that harm women and others who may be disenfranchised by society.

e. Client collaboration and therapist disclosure. Feminist therapy shares the premise of humanist therapy in that therapy ought to be client-centered. Clients ought to be full participants regarding the goals and direction of therapy. This would entail providing clients enough information about the overall and specific goals of therapy, as well as respecting clients' ability to make informed decisions about what is best for them. Also, therapists are encouraged to be candid with clients about what their values are regarding matters related to the clients' gender, ethnicity, sexual orientation, and social circumstances. Clients ought to have such explicit information about their therapist so they can decide if they wish to continue working with the therapist.

Many of the values associated with feminist therapy can be applied judiciously to other clients who, like women, have experienced historical or ongoing oppression, such as LG clients and families. Below is an example of a case that portrays how some premises of feminist therapy can be applied to LG families. The example illustrates how the therapist utilized an eclectic approach to therapy guided by feminist theory to proactively affirm homosexuality in his treatment of the family. The eclectic approach draws on various therapeutic techniques from one or a combination of traditional approaches in order to help a client resolve a conflict or obtain a reduction in symptoms of distress. The technique(s) employed depends on the client's presenting problems, emotional status, and personality style (Wolfe & Goldfried, 1988).

For example, a psychodynamic tactic may include exploring events from a previous time in the client's life (particularly childhood) that may be exacerbating her reaction to current conflicts. Explorations of this nature may lead to insight and self-discovery that ultimately may temper a client's reaction to current stressors. A form of behavioral therapy may include assigning a mutually agreed-upon "homework" to a client and instructing her to reward herself if she successfully performs the assignment. Using a cognitive-based intervention, the therapist may challenge a woman's rigid adherence to beliefs or "rules" that influence her actions, yet cause her unnecessary stress. Finally, the humanistic or client-centered approach–which overlaps considerably with feminist-therapeutic approaches–might entail reaffirming the inherent value of the client and validating her experiences, including her interpretation of her experiences. Any or all of these approaches can be implemented and fused with the feminist sensibilities discussed previously.

The case below involves a lesbian couple who had sought family therapy with the first author (C.N.) to address concerns related to their two children. We consider in this case the couple's goals for seeking treatment, the challenges related to their situation, the conceptualization of the presenting concerns by the couple, and the general direction of treatment. The goal in describing this case is to highlight how therapists can support LG couples and their families as they endeavor to provide a nurturing and stable environment for themselves and their children amid the challenges stemming from living in a society that generally is unsupportive and unaccepting of this particular diverse family constellation.

THE CASE OF THE GARCIA-DAVENPORT FAMILY

Martha Garcia and Cynthia Davenport were in their early 40s and had been in a committed relationship with each other for 15 years. Martha was a computer consultant for an accounting firm, and Cynthia was a nurse at a local hospital. In addition to being lesbians, Martha was Mexican American and Cynthia was non-Hispanic White. Martha and Cynthia reported that although they had struggled on occasion with cultural misunderstandings during the first year of their relationship, they characterized the current status of their relationship as "strong, with minimal conflict." When the two had announced to their parents that they were in love and planned on moving in together, Cynthia's mother was fairly supportive of her daughter's situation (Cynthia's father was deceased). In contrast, Martha described her parents' reaction to her announcement about being a lesbian and being in love with Cynthia as "a complete trauma for the family." Being traditional Mexican Americans and Catholic, her parents were in disbelief over their daughter's sexual orientation and quickly blamed themselves for having failed her as parents.

The therapist asked Martha what the current status was regarding her relationship with her parents. She stated that, today, although her parents are not completely pleased with her sexual orientation or with her relationship with Cynthia, they no longer get into emotionally-charged discussions with her about her life-style. She also indicated that her parents avoid, to the extent that they can, mentioning her to others because " . . . they're afraid the other person will start asking questions about me or my life-style. They're also afraid of losing friends."

At the time therapy was initiated, Martha and Cynthia had two children. Their oldest son, Samuel, was 10, and their youngest daughter, Susan, was six. They reported that they sought therapy because they had various concerns about their children's development, especially Samuel's, given that he would be entering adolescence within a few years. Martha and Cynthia had questions about how to deal with some of the situations their children would increasingly encounter at school and elsewhere about having two mothers. Although Samuel's classmates had in the earlier grades asked why he had two mothers, they seemed to be unphased by Samuel's family structure, likely because of their relatively young ages. However, Martha and Cynthia suspected that as Samuel progressed to higher grades, his classmates' previously benign curiosity may become more aggressive in nature. The therapist asked them if any of Samuel's classmates had already responded negatively to them about their family status. Cynthia stated that recently, a boy had made the comment that "Sam's parents were a couple of Lesbians." When asked how Sam responded, Cynthia stated that "Sam said he felt a little uncomfortable, but did not respond to the kid."

The therapist probed Cynthia and Martha by asking them how it felt to hear what the classmate had said to Sam and about how Sam had reacted. Martha indicated that the classmate's statement made her angry and that she was disappointed that Samuel did not "stick up for his family." The therapist stated, "It would make most parents in your situation feel angry. (Pause . . .). By the same token, it may be an unnecessarily heavy burden on Samuel to expect him to 'battle society' in defense of his parents or family." Cynthia then stated, "We have spent considerable time in the past explaining to Sam the idea that society is the one with the problem of bigotry." The therapist responded, "That's an excellent way to help your children reframe situations involving negative comments by other students at school. In light of that, I think Samuel exercised good judgment by not being dragged into a discussion that might not have been productive. I'm actually pleased with Sam's judgment."

Martha and Cynthia reported that they had agreed early on in their relationship that they would adopt a policy of honesty when their children began asking them questions about sex, and sexuality in general, and about their status as a lesbian couple in particular. They stated that that approach, however, was easier in theory, but more challenging in practice. They expressed reservations about whether such honesty was in their children's best interest. Cynthia stated, "After all, heterosexual couples never have to explain to their children why they are of the opposite sex, or even why they are heterosexual, so why should we have to explain these things to our children?" The therapist shared with them that Cynthia's position may be correct theoretically, but her children likely would benefit from having more, rather than less, information about relationships, including relationships that differ from societal expectations of relationships. (Pause . . .). He stated, "I'm just curious (pause . . .), is there a chance that your recent reluctance to discuss the situation regarding your sexuality with your children reflects some of your own discomfort with your situation?"

Another focus of therapy centered on their relationship between them and their parents and extended family members. According to the couple, their children have a close relationship with Cynthia's mother and extended family (e.g., aunts and uncles and her brother). On Martha's side of the family, the situation was less than optimum. Martha described her father's approach to their children as "friendly, but simultaneously aloof." The status with other family members was mixed. Some of her siblings and aunts and uncles outwardly accepted Martha's lifestyle, partner, and children, whereas other family members, such as one brother and most of her family on her father's side minimized their contact with them. Martha stated that, "Although I wished all of my family would accept us, I'm not bothered by the ones who don't. I'm most concerned over how Samuel and Susan will react when they one day register that some of their cousins may have little interest in being with them."

The last area of concern raised by the two women was related to their ethnicity. Four years into their relationship, Martha and Cynthia had decided to have their first child through artificial insemination. Based on multiple considerations, Martha had elected to carry the baby whose father was a mutual friend of theirs and happened to be non-Hispanic White. As a result, Samuel is biethnic (part Mexican American and part White). Susan was adopted when she was 11 months old and both biological parents were non-Hispanic White. The couple, but particularly Martha, indicated that it was important to them that both children appreciated their parents' respective cultures and that Samuel adopt a healthy attitude about being biethnic.

Case Conceptualization and Interventions

Martha's and Cynthia's situation is one in which two women had maintained a relatively stable, close-knit relationship for 15 years and were in the process of rearing two children, one of whom was close to entering the adolescent stage. Their concerns consisted of knowing how best to prepare their children (especially Samuel) for individuals who either criticize, insult, or reject them because of their parents' lesbianism, maximizing their relationships with family and extended family members who were not fully accepting of them, and facilitating the children's appreciation and pride of their parents' distinct ethnic backgrounds, and in the case of Samuel, his biethnicity.

The therapist treated this couple for four sessions. In only one of the sessions were Samuel and Susan present. Consistent with the feminist notion that therapists ought to disclose their values to their clients, the therapist communicated to Martha and Cynthia that his opinion about homosexuality in general was based on the empirical literature that repeatedly has found nothing inherently pathological about being lesbian or gay. As a means of validating and respecting their experiences, he shared with them that having a lesbian or gay life-style was equally valid as a heterosexual life-style and that he affirmed the right of individuals to be gay or lesbian. He stated, "I celebrate human diversity in all of its manifestations." His disclosure of these views alleviated any anxiety the couple might have had about whether their therapist would genuinely be supportive of them and their situation.

Martha was not pleased with the way their son, Samuel, had chosen to deal with a classmate who had made a mild, but nonetheless disparaging remark about his parents' lesbianism. The therapist validated Martha's anger by universalizing her sentiment (i.e., informing her that most parents in her situation likely would be angered). Using Cynthia's statement about the classmate's comment reflecting society's problem with LG people, the therapist reinforced that idea, which seemed to lower Martha's defenses surrounding that incident. As feminist theory posits, many problems experienced by women–and in this case, by LG people–have their roots in the social environment with which many clients must contend. In this same context, although Cynthia's family was relatively accepting of LG families, Martha's parents and extended family were, in various degrees, products of their own cultural and socioeconomic backgrounds and biases. Highlighting this for the couple served to promote the idea that Martha, Cynthia, and the children should avoid personalizing the indifference that some of Martha's family manifest toward them. In this sense, they were empowered to choose not to accept responsibility for the prejudice held by others. This idea surfaced with Samuel's manner of ignoring his classmate. Litovich and Langhout (2004) delineated this type of empowerment as an effective coping strategy that relieves children from the burden of defending homosexuality or their family.

As an example of being attentive to the language of women, the therapist was sensitive to Cynthia's questioning of why they were obligated to explain their life-style to their children when heterosexuals typically did not have the need to address this with their children. After validating her point, he gently asked her if her recent reluctance to discuss their sexual orientation with their children reflected some of her own discomfort with her situation. This led to a discussion of some of her own residual internalized homophobia.

During the one session with Samuel and Susan, after asking a series of benign questions as a means to establish rapport, the therapist stated, "I think your parents have discussed with you in the past how in society, there are many different types of families." He proceeded to address the fact that some individuals, for different reasons, struggle to accept others solely because they are different. He made the comparison between some individuals' struggle to accept racial or ethnic groups with others who struggle to accept LG families and individuals. The children were already fairly well-versed, based on their parents' discussions and even their school's curriculum, in the inappropriateness and inherent unfairness of society's racial bigotry. This analogy of oppression–if presented in a way that is accessible to children–can help guide their understanding of heterosexism and homophobia. Children's preexisting foundation about racism and its insidious consequences can lay the basis for appreciating the equally toxic consequences of heterosexism. This also reinforces the notion that being gay or lesbian is not inherently problematic, but it is society that has a problem with sexual (and ethnic) minorities.

The therapist took advantage of this segment of the session to address the children's mixed-ethnic parentage and Samuel's biethnicity. The therapist (who coincidently is biethnic) discussed the positive qualities of the two cultures. He also highlighted some benefits of being or living in a mixed-ethnic family. Some examples he shared with them were having opportunities to interact with members of multiple heritages, being able to enjoy diverse customs and celebrations, being able to appreciate situations from a broader perspective, and learning tolerance for diverse social groups and individuals (Negy, Klein, & Brantley, 2004).

CLINICAL IMPLICATIONS AND RECOMMENDATIONS

LG couples and their families–like couples/families of all backgrounds–are comprised of individuals first and foremost, and clinicians must always be cognizant of this as they endeavor to provide the most effective form of treatment to them (Negy, 2004). Therapists, for example, ought not to approach LG couples/families with stereotypes they may have about LG couples/families (in either direction), and they cannot assume that the reason(s) LG couples/families are seeking therapy is related, either directly or indirectly, to their LG status. LG couples/families, like other couples/families, often seek therapy for a wide variety of reasons that have no relation to their sexual orientation. A competent therapist is one who listens well and allows clients to define their problems and concerns as they perceive them to be (Lopez, 1997).

With those caveats in mind, we offer some recommendations to consider when providing therapeutic services to LG couples/families that therapists may find useful. These recommendations are consistent with feminist sensibilities. They include:

- Identify strengths in LG couple and family clients. For example, most LG couples who have children have made extraordinary efforts to obtain them and to rear them, and usually have done so because of their profound love for children. Reinforce the parents' desire and willingness to provide a stable, loving environment to their children, despite the obstacles they face living in a less-than-hospitable society toward LG people.
- Therapists should disclose their favorable and supportive views about diversity, particularly in the context of homosexuality, and affirm the idea that a LG life-style is a valid life-style. It is therapeutic to many LG couples and families to hear a professional in the position of authority declaring unequivocally that diversity is a strength and asset to be cherished. Diversity is beneficial to society because it brings new dimensions to that society's culture and challenges all of us to consciously examine our beliefs and to become more sensitive and compassionate with others who may differ from ourselves.

- Therapists should display genuine respect for LG couples and families. In part, this can be achieved by abstaining from being judgmental. Also, therapists ought to make extra efforts to self-monitor in order to ensure that they are not applying dominant, heterosexist cultural standards to LG clients' problems and behaviors.
- Therapists ought to clarify for LG couples and families that not all problems for which professional help is sought lie within the individuals seeking therapy. LG couples/families may need assistance in differentiating problems whose origins are intrapsychic or intrafamilial versus problems with an external or societal origin. For example, teasing children for having LG parents reflects a problem with society's ignorance and intolerance, rather than a problem due to having gay parents per se.
- In a related way, LG couples/families may struggle with their status within the context of social relationships, and may encounter rejection based solely on their LG status, leaving them feeling isolated and possibly embittered. Therapists should validate these feelings and assist their efforts to establish a network of friends and family members who are accepting, understanding and supportive.
- Children being reared in a LG household may have parents who, for various reasons, have not appropriately developed or supported their children's acceptance and appreciation for having LG parents. Sometimes this situation may be due to one or both parents not having fully worked through their own discomfort with their LG status. Therapists must be sensitive to such a situation and offer support to the children, while confronting LG parents about this possibility in a collaborative and non-threatening manner.
- Finally, consistent with feminist theory (Gilligan, 1982), a significant component of therapy should focus on the relationship between the therapist and the LG couple/family. Based on various meta-analyses, some researchers have concluded that the therapist-client relationship is the cornerstone to successful therapy (Horvath & Symonds, 1991; Martin, Garske, & Davis, 2000).

CONCLUSIONS AND FUTURE DIRECTIONS

As the social fabric of the United States continues to diversify, it is likely that more LG individuals will form stable, committed relationships and some may opt to rear children. Thus far, the empirical litera-ture demonstrates that LG couples who have children appear to be equally effective as parents as are heterosexual parents. Moreover, the scant research on children reared by same-sex parents has found that, overall, these children are no more or less emotionally maladjusted as children reared by opposite-sex parents. In fact, on some dimensions, such as sensitivity to discrimination and sociocultural diversity, chil-dren reared in LG families appear to have a better-developed social con-science than comparable children reared by heterosexual parents. In this article, we have attempted to highlight some of the challenges posed by LG parents as they endeavor to provide an optimum family life for their children. Specifically, we have illustrated through the presentation of a clinical case how judicious application of feminist therapy can promote resiliency and psychological well-being among parents and children in LG families.

Although present research does well in delineating differences be-tween LG and heterosexual parents and the effects of LG parenting on their children, much is to be desired from future research. For example, scant research exists regarding gay fathers (Lambert, 2005; Tasker, 2005). Systematic evaluations of the psychological development of children of gay fathers have not been published. Another shortcoming of the current research is that a majority of studies examining LG fami-lies are almost exclusively on White and relatively well-educated popu-lations who are open with their identity. More research is needed about LG families of ethnically diverse backgrounds in order to know how they fare emotionally and socially in light of having multiple minority statuses.

As noted earlier, much research has been influenced by heterosexism and has failed to account for the fluidity and complexity of sexual orien-tation definitions (e.g., relying solely on self-identification to establish homosexuality; Tasker, 2005). A battery of questions should be utilized to examine in more detail the variability in sexual identification of both parents and their children (Tasker, 2005). Additionally, the impact of adopting a child-centered approach versus the primacy of the couple dyad should be investigated along with examining how the flexibility and adaptability of LG families contribute to the development of rela-tionships (Lynch, 2000). Future research must expand upon the current views of LG families and experiment with approaches other than defi-cit-comparison models. Such models limit research by leaving diversity and strengths in LG parenting underexplored and under-appreciated.

REFERENCES

Avis, J. (1987). Deepening awareness: A private study guide to feminism and family therapy. *Journal of Psychotherapy and the Family, 3*(4), 15-45.

Broverman, I. K., Broverman, D. M., & Clarkson, F. E. (1970). Sex role stereotypes and clinical judgment of mental health. *Journal of Consulting and Clinical Psychology, 34,* 1-7.

Clunis, D. M., & Green, G. D. (1995). *The lesbian parenting book: A guide to creating families and raising children.* Seattle, WA: Seal Press.

Connolly, C. M. (2005). A qualitative exploration of resilience in long-term lesbian couples. *The Family Journal: Counseling and Therapy for Couples and Families, 13,* 266-280.

Eldridge, N. S., & Barrett, S. E. (2003). Biracial lesbian-led adoptive families. In L. B. Silverstein & T. J. Goodrich (Eds.), *Feminist family therapy: Empowerment in social context* (pp. 307-318). Washington, DC: American Psychological Association.

Fredriksen-Goldsen, K. I., & Erera, P. L. (2003). Lesbian-headed stepfamilies. *Journal of Human Behavior in the Social Environment, 8,* 171-187.

Gilligan, C. (1982). *In a different voice: Psychological theory and women's development.* Cambridge, MA: Harvard University Press.

Golombok, S., Perry, B., Burston, A., Murray, C., Mooney-Somers, J., Stevens, M., & Golding, J. (2003). Children with lesbian parents: A community study. *Developmental Psychology, 39,* 20-33.

Halstead, K. (2003). Over the rainbow: The lesbian family. In L. B. Silverstein & T. J. Goodrich (Eds.), *Feminist family therapy: Empowerment in social context* (pp. 39-50). Washington, DC: American Psychological Association.

Hare-Mustin, R. (1978). A feminist approach to family therapy. *Family Process, 17,* 181-194.

Hequembourg, A. (2004). Unscripted motherhood: Lesbian mothers negotiating incompletely institutionalized family relationships. *Journal of Social and Personal Relationships, 21,* 739-762.

Hill, M., & Ballou, M. (1998). Making therapy feminist: A practice survey. *Women & Therapy, 21,* 1-16.

Horvath, A. O., & Symonds, B. D. (1991). Relation between working alliance and outcome in psychotherapy: A meta-analysis. *Journal of Counseling Psychology, 38,* 139-149.

Krestan, J. A., & Bepko, C. S. (1980). The problem of fusion in the lesbian relationship. *Family Process, 19,* 277-389.

Lambert, S. (2005). Gay and lesbian families: What we know and where to go from here. *The Family Journal: Counseling and Therapy for Couples and Families, 13,* 43-51.

Litovich, M. L., & Langhout, M. D. (2004). Framing heterosexism in lesbian families: A preliminary examination of resilient coping. *Journal of Community and Applied Social Psychology, 14,* 411-435.

Lopez, S. R. (1997). Cultural competence in psychotherapy: A guide for clinicians and their supervisors. In C. E. Watkins, Jr. (Ed.), *Handbook of psychotherapy supervision* (pp. 570-588). New York: John Wiley & Sons, Inc.

Lynch, J. M. (2000). Considerations of family structure and gender composition: The lesbian and gay stepfamily. *Journal of Homosexuality, 40,* 81-95.

MacCallum, F., & Golombok, S. (2004). Children raised in fatherless families from infancy: A follow-up of children of lesbian and single heterosexual mothers at early adolescence. *Journal of Child Psychology and Psychiatry, 45,* 1407-1419.

Martin, D. J., Garske, J. P., & Davis, M. K. (2000). Relation of the therapeutic relation with outcome and other variables. A meta-analytic review. *Journal of Consulting and Clinical Psychology, 68,* 438-450.

McGoldrick, M., Anderson, C. M., & Walsh, F. (1989). Women in families and family therapy. In M. McGoldrick, C. M. Anderson, & F. Walsh (Eds.), *Women in families: A framework for family therapy* (pp. 3-15). New York: Norton.

Negy, C. (2004). Therapy with dissimilar clients: Issues to consider along this road more traveled. In C. Negy (Ed.), *Cross-cultural psychotherapy: Toward a critical understanding of diverse clients* (pp. 3-22). Reno, NV: Bent Tree Press.

Negy, C., Klein, J. L, & Brantley, E. D. C. (2004). Multiracial/ethnic clients: History, models, and clinical implications. In C. Negy (Ed.), *Cross-cultural psychotherapy: Toward a critical understanding of diverse clients* (pp. 231-246). Reno, NV: Bent Tree Press.

Oswald, R. F. (2002). Resilience within family networks of lesbians and gay men: Intentionality and redefinition. *Journal of Marriage and Family, 64,* 374-383.

Park, S. M. (2004). Feminism and therapy. In C. Negy (Ed.), *Cross-cultural psychotherapy: Toward a critical understanding of diverse clients* (pp. 281-300). Reno, NV: Bent Tree Press.

Prouty, A. (2001). Experiencing feminist family therapy supervision. *Journal of Feminist Family Therapy, 12,* 171-203.

Tasker, F. (2005). Lesbian mothers, gay fathers, and their children: A review. *Journal of Developmental and Behavioral Pediatrics, 26,* 224-240.

Vanfraussen, K., Ponjaert-Kristoffersen, I., & Brewaeys, A. (2003). Family functioning in lesbian families created by donor insemination. *American Journal of Orthopsychiatry, 73,* 78-90.

Walters, M., Carter, B., Papp, P., & Silverstein, O. (1988). Toward a feminist perspective in family therapy. In M. Walters, B. Carter, P. Papp, & O. Silverstein (Eds.), *The invisible web: Gender patterns in family relationships* (pp. 15-30). New York: The Guilford Press.

Wolfe, B. E., & Goldfried, M. R. (1988). Research on psychotherapy integration: Recommendations and conclusions from an NIMH workshop. *Journal of Consulting and Clinical Psychology, 56,* 448-451.

doi:10.1300/J086v18n01_03

Intimate Violence Among Lesbian Couples: Emerging Data and Critical Needs

Bette Speziale
Cynthia Ring

SUMMARY. Intimate violence between opposite sex partners has been increasingly acknowledged and empirically studied in recent decades. Findings from both quantitative and qualitative research have resulted in a substantive knowledge base that is widely accepted and applied in treatment. Unfortunately, intimate violence between partners of the same sex has not been adequately addressed. The limited research data that has emerged raises questions not only about the prevalence of the problem, but also the definition of the problem, some differing dynamics as compared to heterosexual couples. the responses of crisis workers, social services, the police, and the courts, and appropriate therapeutic interventions. The authors discuss the above mentioned topics as they apply to intimate violence between female partners. They offer recommendations for clinicians who treat women involved in abusive, intimate relationships, as well as researchers who aim to build much needed knowledge about this neglected issue. doi:10.1300/J086v18n01_04 *[Article copies available for a fee from The Haworth Document Delivery Service: 1-800-HAWORTH. E-mail address: <docdelivery@haworthpress.com> Website: <http://www.HaworthPress.com> © 2006 by The Haworth Press, Inc. All rights reserved.]*

KEYWORDS. Partner abuse, family violence, couples, couple violence, lesbian, women

[Haworth co-indexing entry note]: "Intimate Violence Among Lesbian Couples: Emerging Data and Critical Needs." Speziale, Bette, and Cynthia Ring. Co-published simultaneously in *Journal of Feminist Family Therapy* (The Haworth Press, Inc.) Vol. 18, No. 1/2, 2006, pp. 85-96; and: *Lesbian Families' Challenges and Means of Resiliency: Implications for Feminist Family Therapy* (ed: Anne M. Prouty Lyness) The Haworth Press, Inc., 2006, pp. 85-96. Single or multiple copies of this article are available for a fee from The Haworth Document Delivery Service [1-800-HAWORTH, 9:00 a.m. - 5:00 p.m. (EST). E-mail address: docdelivery@haworthpress.com].

INTRODUCTION

From a couple and family systems perspective, the partnerships of many lesbian women appear to be quite functional (Speziale & Gopalakrishna, 2004). However, as with heterosexual couples, the critical issue of violence is a reality that professionals need to understand. Grounded in the academic literature, this article offers an overview of intimate partner abuse among lesbian women including emerging data about prevalence and behavioral characteristics, as well as responses of law enforcement and social service providers. In addition, the authors discuss implications of the current knowledge of this pressing social problem for clinicians and researchers who address situations of lesbian partner abuse.

PREVALENCE OF LESBIAN PARTNER ABUSE

Empirical findings about the prevalence of violence among lesbian partners vary. West (2002) conducted a review of research studies for reported rates. She found that approximately 30-40% of lesbian women have been involved in at least one, if not more, physically abusive relationships. The forms of physical abuse that were most common were slapping, pushing, and shoving. Physical beatings and assaults with weapons also occurred, but less often. Rates of sexual violence, which included experiences of coerced kissing and fondling, as well as vaginal, anal, and oral penetration, ranged widely from 7% to 55%. By far, the most common types of partner abuse were verbal and psychological with a reported rate of over 80%.

Other experts have reported types of abuse that are less frequently addressed in studies of violence between lesbian partners. A study by Renzetti (1992) included child abuse and pet abuse by one's partner. She found that among couples who lived with children or pets, the perpetrators abused the partner's children in almost 30% of cases, and abused pets in approximately 38% of cases. In the same study, Renzetti also reported particular types of abuse germane to lesbian women with disabilities. For example, there were women who reported being left by a partner in high-risk, dangerous circumstances without help or the means to escape. A diabetic participant reported being forced to ingest sugar, consequently suffering high risk of a medical crisis. A more recent study (Ristock, 2003), based on a sample in which 13% of participants were women with disabilities, found that these women endured more physical abuse than verbal or psychological abuse. The vulnerability of women with disabilities to stronger, more powerful, able-bodied partners was apparent.

Some researchers (Kuehnle & Sullivan, 2003; West, 2002) assert that the prevalence of partner abuse in lesbian relationships is comparable to that of heterosexual relationships. Furthermore, the underreporting of abuse that occurs with heterosexual couples likely also occurs with same-sex couples. Therefore, rates are probably higher than documented. But other academics do not concur. Citing such issues as inadequate racial and ethnic diversity in samples, the reliance on self-reporting, the diverse operational definitions of violence, and the lack of sociocultural context, they claim that it is difficult to arrive at precise rates as well as comparisons with partner abuse in heterosexual relationships (Girshick, 2002; Ristock, 2003). Nevertheless, contrary to some feminists' claim that women are not violent in their relationships with each other, there does appear to be a consensus that same-sex partner abuse is a serious and inadequately addressed dysfunction in couple and family systems.

BEHAVIORAL CHARACTERISTICS

Conflicts over a number of issues, including alcohol and drug use, unemployment, finances, household responsibilities, emotional intimacy, and sexual behavior contribute to abuse among lesbian couples (Lockhart, White, Causby, & Isaac, 1994; Schilit, Lie, & Montagne, 1990). Alcohol, in particular, has been identified as a major risk factor because bars catering exclusively to lesbian women are a common environment in which to socialize (West, 2002).

Although contributing factors involved in lesbian partner abuse appear similar to those that are involved with heterosexual partners' abuse, there are some distinct aspects of couple system functioning. Characteristic of lesbian relationships is fusion. As Slater (1995) explains in her discussion of the lesbian family life cycle, fusion has been equated with merging or enmeshment, concepts that have negative connotations when referring to couple and family systems functioning. But fusion, briefly defined as the intense emotional closeness and high level of interdependence between intimate partners, is not necessarily problematic in lesbian relationships. When it helps partners cope with the assaults of a hostile, unsupportive social environment, it can be a source of strength and resilience. In contrast, when it obstructs the ongoing development of both partners' individual identities, as well as their relationship over the life course, then it no longer serves a protective function. As Slater (1995) aptly observes, fusion becomes dysfunctional when it begins to limit involvement in friendships and separate activities, as well as hinders genuine differences in behavior and communication.

Lockhart et al. (1994) concur. Among their research participants fusion seemed to fuel the violence. Some abusers saw their partners' friendships as a form of personal rejection, and therefore interpreted them as major threats to their intimate relationships. Others became aggressive when attempting to extricate themselves from frustrating, fused relationships. In general, both internal and external boundary issues inherent in such relationships put couples at risk for violence.

Another consideration is that of power skews in relationships. Ristock's (2003) findings from a multisite study in Canada were particularly revealing of diverse dynamics. Consistent with the classic scenario of domestic violence that has been delineated with heterosexual couples, there were lesbian couples who enacted this same pattern of roles and phases. The perpetrator seeks to maintain power and control over the victim and uses various tactics in a cycle of violence (i.e., building of tension, enactment of abuse, pseudo reconciliation, building of tension, etc.). Ristock (2003) acknowledges Tully's (2001) work envisioning a spiral of violence that, although framed differently, is somewhat comparable, and recognizes the outcomes of reconciliation or escalation and explosion.

However, Ristock (2003) also discovered that the conventional pattern did not suffice to explain the power dynamics in all lesbian relationships. Participants in her study described what she termed shifting power dynamics and scenarios of violence in which one could not easily dichotomize perpetrator and victim. In these cases the roles fluctuated, and the alleged cycle or spiral of violence was less predictable. Motives, too, were difficult to discern, that is, whether one partner was fighting back to fend off injury or fighting back to retaliate and hurt one's partner. Roles and motives could also shift with the same person in subsequent relationships.

A particularly powerful weapon of abuse among same-sex partners is that of forced outing. It can occur in same-sex relationships when one partner is out-of-the-closet and the other is not. The partner who is out threatens to or actually discloses her closeted partner's status to family, friends, colleagues, supervisors and others in positions of authority and power. Such a disclosure can have tremendous consequences for the individual's psychological and social well-being, personal and professional relationships, as well as employment, career, and finances. Sulis (1999) notes that bisexual women in same-sex abusive relationships are highly vulnerable, especially if they have children. The fear of losing custody of one's children can inhibit bisexual women from leaving abusive, same-sex relationships. Moreover, given the controversy surrounding the legitimacy of bisexuality as a sexual orientation and the concomitant politics in the lesbian community, bisexual women can become targets of psychological, verbal, and even physical abuse from that sector.

Another consideration regarding power skews in lesbian relationships emanates from a particular finding unique to Ristock's (2003) research. Almost half of the participants reported that their first same-sex relationship was abusive. In these cases the abusive partner was usually older and had been out-of-the-closet longer. She was also likely to have a history of aggression and seemed to prey on younger, inexperienced women who were just coming out. In this study she was referred to as a serial abuser, a lesbian woman who had abused her partner in most or all of her sexual relationships.

As a seasoned, qualitative researcher Ristock (2002) aptly observes that couples' interpersonal behavior and dynamics must be understood in the context of larger social systems and social forces such as homophobia, isolation, and invisibility of lesbian women and couples. As she admonishes from interpretation of her research participants' lived experiences of intimate partner violence:

> Given this diversity of women's accounts, it is important to closely examine the specific contexts and spaces in which violence occurs so that we can make distinctions between situations that will help us in our efforts to eradicate violence. Efforts to understand violence in lesbian relationships that ignore these contexts run the risk of treating all cases of relationship violence as equivalent and interchangeable, when that does not seem to be the case. Further, ignoring social contexts depoliticizes our analysis of violence by glossing over the social inequities that put people at risk. (p. 58)

RESPONSES OF LAW ENFORCEMENT
AND SOCIAL SERVICES

The first proactive behavior among most abused women is a crisis call to the police. However, the expectation of help is not consistently realized with lesbian women. In Rose's (2003) study of community interventions in cases of intimate partner violence as well as incidents of homophobic violence against lesbians, hotline calls and responses were investigated. Findings revealed that police responses were hostile or inadequate in many cases. Another study of lesbians, and gays' reporting practices (Kuehnle & Sullivan, 2003) found that lesbian victims who reported incidents to the police experienced diverse responses. In some cases police refused to take complaints, in some cases victims were arrested, and in others the offenders were arrested. In the same study, lesbian women were slightly more likely than gay men to file incident reports of intimate partner violence with the police, but usually when former husbands were involved.

When abuse by lesbian partners progresses to the stage of court hearings, problems at the meso-system level become apparent. Burke, Jordan, and Owen (2002) found in their study that seven states did not allow same-sex partners to apply for domestic violence protection orders. In three other states, sodomy statutes could be used to require that gay men and lesbian women admit to illegal sexual behavior in order to qualify for protection orders. And in many states, where courts are mandated by law to accept a heterosexual person's petition for protection, lesbian women's as well as gay men's petitions are solely at the discretion of the court. In this study only four states allowed for equal protection of same-sex partners in domestic violence situations.

According to Fray-Witzer (1999), there are some states that actually define domestic violence as that which occurs between spouses, former spouses, or family members. This type of definition clearly excludes lesbian and gay couples. Furthermore, in cases of sexual assault of one woman by another, patriarchal definitions and heterosexist stereotyping also have consequences. As Girshick (2002) has asserted, even the rape and sexual assault statutes operate on the fundamental premise of opposite sex partners and penile penetration of a vagina. According to this supposed logic, a female cannot commit sexual violence against another female, and lesbian women's claims to the contrary are neither credible nor legitimate. Although revised rape and domestic violence laws have incorporated gender neutral language, this reform does not suffice. In application, these changes merely allow for role reversal in heterosexual couples (i.e., female perpetrators and male victims), rather than extending protections to lesbian and gay couples. As Girshick (2002) observes:

> The legal system uses this gendered view to understand domestic violence and rape, and police officers, judges, juries, and attorneys listen to these cases with this subtext in mind. Consequently, when lesbians and bisexual women tell of battering and rape, they tell a story with a different gender scheme, one that is at odds with the existing heterosexist subtext. (p. 144)

Despite official position statements of support for same-sex couples and their families (NASW, 2003), social service agencies and social workers remain inconsistent with their interventions and resources. Kuehnle & Sullivan (2003) found that most battered women's shelters do not provide services to abused lesbian women, nor are their staff members educated and trained to manage situations of violence between same-sex couples. Likewise, Fray-Witzer (1999) discovered that many battered women's programs refuse service to lesbian women, and do not have a basic knowledge and understanding of the issues involved. Moreover, even those agencies allegedly providing services to lesbian women appear to display some discrepancies in their policies and practices. In Renzetti's (1996) survey of over 1500 domestic violence service programs, 96% claimed that they welcomed lesbians as clients. However, just over 9% actually engaged in activities like advertising in the media and lesbian/gay newspapers, distributing brochures on lesbian battering, and providing support groups for battered lesbians. The researcher observed that even if shelters and social service organizations were inclined to serve abused lesbian women, they feared a loss of both individual and institutional funding if they did, or if they publicized such services. In the current societal context of the ongoing battle for legal recognition and protection of same-sex partnerships, her explanation appears valid.

Ristock's (2003) use of focus groups with feminist service providers revealed some dilemmas in practice. Participants were discovering that the approaches that they applied to heterosexual couples did not seem to meet the needs of same-sex couples. Not only did they begin to reconsider the premises on which they based their practice and programming, but they also began reconsidering what they would define as an unhealthy but not abusive relationship.

Surprisingly, even agencies serving the LGBT community are not always sources of help. One study found that most of their anti-violence programs and resources assist victims of hate crimes rather than partner abuse (Burke, Jordan, & Owen, 2002). However, one must exercise caution in interpreting such findings. Agencies serving the LGBT community exclusively are not all providers of a full range of social services, in particular, crisis intervention and clinical services, nor are they all staffed by licensed social workers and therapists. Therefore, it may be necessary to determine an agency's mission and related program services before assuming inadequate or indifferent responses to specific types of violence.

DISCUSSION AND IMPLICATIONS

Academics are not oblivious to the fact that empirical investigations of sensitive subjects with marginalized persons like members of the LGBT population carry heavy ethical responsibilities, particularly because they are conducted in an ever-changing and hostile sociopolitical environment (Martin & Meezan, 2003). But as daunting as such endeavors may be, it is necessary to undertake them. The research on violence in the intimate relationships of female partners is limited. Additional studies must be conducted to fill the gaps in our knowledge base, as well as to inform much-needed professional and continuing education in this area. The consistency in research findings to date (Alexander, 2002), as well as the clinical experience of couple and family therapists (Istar, 1996; Slater, 1995), clearly point to the urgency in addressing the problem. The consequences of continuing to ignore and trivialize same-sex partner abuse are serious, not only for the physical and mental health, social well-being, and very lives of the women who find themselves in such crisis situations, but also for the children that they parent. Moreover, it is challenging for therapists and other professionals to address major dysfunction in same-sex couples' relationships competently and effectively when these relationships are not socially and legally recognized. Current political and legislative agendas aimed at passing state laws defining marriage as a legal relationship between a man and a woman, and prohibiting civil unions, do not bode well for the future of committed, same-sex couples or the eradication of violence. Not only do such laws deny partners the ordinary entitlements provided heterosexual couples in our society, but they also, unwittingly, perpetuate and escalate violence within the relationships and nuclear families of same-sex couples. As has been previously noted, states vary tremendously in their laws and the courts' interpretation and application to actual situations (Fray-Witzer, 1999; Girshick, 2002). And without equal protection of the law, prevention, treatment, and intervention efforts by therapists, social services providers, and law enforcement are severely impeded.

In spite of the political and legal obstacles, clinicians willing to serve female partners involved in violent relationships can begin to make inroads. Mandated clients will not be referred by the courts in many geographical locales, but some clients will present voluntarily. However, clinicians should not expect them to define their problems as abuse or violence. Frequently, they will deny abuse and identify their concerns as depression, anxiety, or relationship issues (Girshick, 2003; Istar, 1996; Ristock, 2003). Nonetheless, the first priority, as in all crisis prevention and intervention, is the safety of the persons involved. Clinicians must conduct a rapid assessment of the persons and their situation to determine imminent danger to self and others in the immediate environment (Roberts, 2000). Where the potential exists for fatal or severe injury to the person, partner, children or other household members, referrals to shelters or safe houses may be necessary. However, in view of what research data suggests about the paucity of community resources, it may be difficult to find such services in many locales. Therefore, it is essential that therapists, counselors, and social workers be aware of which organizations in their communities provide services to lesbian women and, if necessary, their children. If services are lacking, then seeking safe haven with family members or friends may be a viable option. Clinicians must remember that researchers have reported inadequate and sometimes hostile responses from police officers, crisis hotline workers, and established programs, even in the LGBT sector. Compounding this dilemma is the fact that few women will have access to legal recourse within the courts. Therefore, in helping clients to devise a safety plan, informal support systems may be the only option in a crisis.

If there is no risk of imminent danger, Istar (1996) suggests that, whenever possible, initial assessment should include both female partners. A couple system assessment is an advantage over that of an individual assessment. As our current knowledge demonstrates, the classic scenario with its clearly defined, dichotomous roles of perpetrator and victim is sometimes but not always the reality. Listening to both women and observing their interactions can be revealing of relational roles, boundaries, level of fusion, and the balance of power, as well as the context and types of abuse that may be occurring. Thorough initial assessment can also aid in determining whether the clinician may proceed with couple therapy, or whether each partner would be better served by an alternative treatment. The latter path is clearly needed, for example, when alcohol or drug dependency is evident.

Istar's (1996) recommendation counters current thinking among couple and family therapists who assert that, whenever abuse is present, the least risky and best practice is to treat partners separately. However, couple assessment and couple therapy can have other distinct advantages with female partners. The therapist can affirm bonds between women and convey support of their committed relationship, thereby negating society's meta-message that their partnership and family system are deviant and inherently destructive to themselves and others. As Istar (1996) notes from her clinical experience, refusal to conduct couple therapy may result in female clients' termination of treatment and, consequently, the seeking out of professionals who are neither culturally sensitive to the issues that committed women confront, nor affirming of families headed by same-sex couples. By building a trusting and genuinely validating therapeutic relationship with her clients, the affirming clinician is then in a position to help redefine and reframe their presenting problem. Ultimately, clients and therapist can work collaboratively toward ending the violence and developing a healthy and highly functional family system.

Empirical findings from focus groups of feminist domestic violence service providers raised other critical issues about serving intimate female partners (Ristock, 2003). Participants claimed that the knowledge base and interventions commonly used with heterosexual couples did not seem to fit what they were finding with lesbian couples. As previously stated, differences in power dynamics and functioning were apparent and presented challenges in assessment and treatment. Moreover, direct practice experience raised questions about the very definition of partner abuse. In other words, service providers began to question the behavioral boundaries of what constituted an abusive relationship and what constituted an unhealthy relationship.

Such questions are not purely philosophical. Our responses to them have major implications for professional judgments rendered in assessment, intervention, and disposition of cases of intimate partner violence. Although there may be consensus on the more egregious forms of violence between partners, there is still some debate on what might be viewed as normative responses to conflict in an intimate relationship. Even among the most loving couples there are disagreements that can result in insensitive and inappropriate behavior. But when does insensitive and inappropriate transgress boundaries to become cruel and abusive? Definitional parameters, particularly in consideration of behavioral norms and diversity relative to situational context and culture, are still somewhat enigmatic. The emerging data on violence between female partners suggest that the issues may be more complex than originally thought. Therefore, these current questions necessitate not merely more extensive research about intimate partner violence, but also a re-examination of fundamental beliefs, conceptual frameworks, and working models for intervention and treatment.

REFERENCES

Alexander, C. J. (2002). Violence in gay and lesbian relationships. *Journal of Gay & Lesbian Social Services, 14*(1), 95-98.

Burke, T. W., Jordan, M. L., & Owen, S. S. (2002). A cross-national comparison of gay and lesbian domestic violence. *Journal of Contemporary Criminal Justice, 18*(3), 231-257.

Fray-Witzer, E. (1999). Twice abused: Same-sex domestic violence and the law. In B. Leventhal & S. E. Lundy (Eds.), *Same-sex domestic violence: Strategies for change* (pp. 19-41). Thousand Oaks, CA: Sage.

Girshick, L. B. (2002). *Woman-to-woman sexual violence: Does she call it rape?* Boston: Northeastern University Press.

Istar, A. (1996). Couple assessment: Identifying and intervening in domestic violence in lesbian relationships. *Journal of Gay & Lesbian Social Services, 4*(1), 93-106.

Kuehnle, K., & Sullivan, A. (2003). Gay and lesbian victimization: Reporting factors in domestic violence and bias incidents. *Criminal Justice and Behavior, 30*(1), 85-96.

Lockhart, L. L., White, B. W., Causby, V., & Isaac, A. (1994). Letting out the secret: Violence in lesbian relationships. *Journal of Interpersonal Violence, 9*(4), 469-492.

Martin, J. I., & Meezan, W. (2003). Applying ethical standards to research and evaluations involving lesbian, gay, bisexual, and transgender populations. *Journal of Gay & Lesbian Social Services, 15*(1/2), 181-201.

National Association of Social Workers (NASW) (2003). *Social work speaks* (6th ed.). Washington, DC: Author.

Renzetti, C. M. (1992). *Violent betrayal: Partner abuse in lesbian relationships.* Newbury Park, CA: Sage Publications.

Renzetti, C. M. (1996). The poverty of services for battered lesbians. *Journal of Gay & Lesbian Social Services, 4*(1), 61-68.

Ristock, J. L. (2002). *No more secrets: Violence in lesbian relationships.* New York: Routledge.

Ristock, J. L. (2003). Exploring dynamics of abusive lesbian relationships: Preliminary analysis of a multisite, qualitative study. *American Journal of Community Psychology, 31*(3/4), 329-341.

Roberts, A. R. (2000). Crisis theory and crisis intervention. In A. R. Roberts (Ed.), *Crisis intervention handbook: Assessment, treatment, and research* (2nd ed.) (pp. 2-30). New York: Oxford University Press.

Rose, S. M. (2003). Community interventions concerning homophobic violence and partner violence against lesbians. *Journal of Lesbian Studies, 7*(4), 125-139.

Schilit, R., Lie, G.-Y., & Montagne, M. (1990). Substance use as a correlate of violence in intimate lesbian relationships. *Journal of Homosexuality, 19*(3), 51-66.

Slater, S. (1995). *The lesbian family life cycle.* New York: The Free Press.

Speziale, B., & Gopalakrishna, V. (2004). Social support and functioning of nuclear families headed by lesbian couples. *AFFILIA: Journal of Women and Social Work, 19*(2), 174-184.

Sulis, S. (1999). Battered bisexual women. In B. Leventhal & S. E. Lundy (Eds.), *Same-sex domestic violence: Strategies for change* (pp. 173-180). Thousand Oaks, CA: Sage.

Tully, C. T. (2001). Domestic violence: The ultimate betrayal of human rights. *Journal of Gay & Lesbian Social Services, 13*(1/2), 83-98.

West, C. M. (2002). Lesbian intimate partner violence: Prevalence and dynamics. *Journal of Lesbian Studies, 6*(1), 121-127.

doi:10.1300/J086v18n01_04

Exploring a Community's Response to Lesbian Domestic Violence Through the Voices of Providers: A Qualitative Study

Suzanne R. Merlis
Deanna Linville

SUMMARY. Lesbian domestic violence has been frequently denied among lesbian communities and society as a whole. As a result, women involved in same-sex abusive relationships remain isolated, fearful, and reluctant to identify and seek help for the abuse. This study investigated a lesbian community's response to domestic violence in same-sex relationships and the factors impacting the response. The participants included fifteen mental health professionals with expertise in the field of lesbian domestic violence. The phenomenon of "lessening the load" emerged as the central theme that categorized the lesbian community's response to domestic violence. Implications for further research and treatment are also discussed. doi:10.1300/J086v18n01_05 *[Article copies available for a fee from The Haworth Document Delivery Service: 1-800-HAWORTH. E-mail address: <docdelivery@haworthpress.com> Website: <http://www.HaworthPress.com> © 2006 by The Haworth Press, Inc. All rights reserved.]*

KEYWORDS. Lesbian couples, domestic violence, partner violence, lesbian community, feminist family therapy, feminist research

[Haworth co-indexing entry note]: "Exploring a Community's Response to Lesbian Domestic Violence Through the Voices of Providers: A Qualitative Study." Merlis, Suzanne R., and Deanna Linville. Co-published simultaneously in *Journal of Feminist Family Therapy* (The Haworth Press, Inc.) Vol. 18, No. 1/2, 2006, pp. 97-136; and: *Lesbian Families' Challenges and Means of Resiliency: Implications for Feminist Family Therapy* (ed: Anne M. Prouty Lyness) The Haworth Press, Inc., 2006, pp. 97-136. Single or multiple copies of this article are available for a fee from The Haworth Document Delivery Service [1-800-HAWORTH, 9:00 a.m. - 5:00 p.m. (EST). E-mail address: docdelivery@haworthpress.com].

Available online at http://jfft.haworthpress.com
doi:10.1300/J086v18n01_05

INTRODUCTION

In the late 1960s, the feminist movement was credited with bringing domestic violence to the attention of the nation as a significant social problem. The first "safe house" for battered women, established in 1971, was in England. The first American shelter for battered women, sponsored by Women's Advocates Minnesota Inc., was opened in 1972. In addition, significant changes have been made in legislative policy around domestic violence (Davidson, 1978; Frieze & Brown, 1987).

Unfortunately, the rates of partner abuse remain very high despite the considerable efforts of researchers and professionals to increase awareness and reduce the frequency of domestic violence. In a report by the Justice of Bureau Statistics (JBS) from 1992-1996 that examined both heterosexual and homosexual domestic violence, eight out of 1000 women and one out of 1000 men were victims of domestic violence. Domestic violence research and treatment have primarily focused on violence in heterosexual couples, specifically men who batter their partners (Peterman & Dixon, 2003). Researching violence within lesbian relationships raises questions that challenge both the existing theories of domestic violence and the understanding of a woman's prescribed role and position in a relationship and society. Historical feminist theory has asserted that gender is a central factor regarding violence. Yet when violence occurs between two woman, issues of socialization, power, control and psychology may need to be evaluated differently because gender may no longer be the central factor in explaining the abuse.

Lesbian, gay, bisexual, and transgender partners experience domestic violence at a rate equal to that of heterosexual relationships (Brand & Kidd, 1986; Fortunata & Kohn, 2003; Peterman & Dixon, 2003). For many, it is difficult to believe that lesbian battering exists. People may find it difficult to fathom that women, who have been socialized to nurture, actually harm other women both physically and emotionally. Acknowledgment may also reinforce homophobic stereotypes and open up the community for further attacks and discrimination by the dominant culture (Benewitz, 1990 as cited by Elliot, 1990; Pharr, 1986; Russo, 1999).

The occurrence of domestic violence cuts across a diverse range of groups. This range has necessitated a shift in the battered women's movement 15-year philosophy of focusing primarily on white, heterosexual domestic violence with male perpetrators and female victims.

Researchers emphasize that the meaning and significance of domestic violence varies across groups because those who are marginalized and those who are members of dominant groups experience and define their domestically violent situations differently (Collins, 1991; Crenshaw, 1994). Additionally, Russo (1999) emphasizes that understanding these differences is central to the recognition of battering outside of its stereotypical heterosexual form.

A debate exists surrounding the question of whether women are as violent as men (Gelles & Loseke, 1993). This debate may serve to undermine the feminist theory of domestic violence and continues to perpetuate a one-dimensional model of violent behavior. Renzetti (1996) argues that intimate violence, as well as the individual and institutionalized responses to that violence, is gender-based. When women use violence, they are accused of behaving "like men." This suggests that women's behavior is being evaluated within established norms of male behavior. The application of this idea to lesbian relationships makes the assumption that the abuser in violent lesbian relationships is playing the masculine role and the victim is playing the feminine role. As a result of these stereotypical gender roles, lesbian partner abuse is misunderstood and victims are often denied help. Research has shown that violent behavior in women is quantitatively and qualitatively different from violent behavior in men, thus documenting gender differences (Renzetti, 1996). Feminist theory emphasizes the importance of including many factors to examine how gender intersects with other status variables (Hirsch & Keller, 1991). Feminist research also focuses on illuminating differences between heterosexual and homosexual battering through a feminist framework emphasizing inequalities such as sexism, heterosexism, racism, and classism.

The Committee on Family Violence of the National Institute of Mental Health (1992) in part defined domestic violence as "acts that are physically and emotionally harmful or that carry the potential to cause physical harm (and) may also include sexual coercion or assaults, physical intimidation, threats to kill or to harm, or restraint of normal activities or freedom, and denial of access to resources" (Burgess & Croswell, 1996). For the purpose of this study, this broad definition of domestic violence will be used because it is inclusive of the experiences of many victims.

There are only a limited number of published empirical reports on lesbian domestic violence (Brand & Kidd, 1986; Warshafsky, 1987; Renzetti, 1988; Coleman, 1990; Russo, 1999) leaving most of the data as anecdotal and descriptive in nature. The anecdotal nature of the existing data is reflective of the strategy of the battered women's movement to listen to the voices of battered women themselves. Survivors have been a tremendous source of information because their testimonies often counteract misconceptions about batterers and abuse (Walber, 1988). Giving voice to women's experiences and addressing issues such as domestic violence in a woman's life have also been an integral part of feminist theory and research (Bloom, 1998). In a similar fashion, it is important to access the knowledge and experience of mental health providers who currently work with lesbians experiencing domestic violence, so that we can understand what services are being provided to the lesbian community and how these services can be improved. In this study, attempts were initially made to seek out the voices of both lesbian survivors and perpetrators along with mental health professionals, but only one survivor came forward. One important factor that emerged in the voices of the mental health professionals we had spoken with was how the professionals and the lesbian community at large appeared to be grappling with how to respond to the prevalence of domestic violence among same-sex female relationships. Although it seemed clear that attempts were being made in the lesbian community to address domestic violence, these attempts had not been successful in enhancing the ability of and access to services. Our predicament of locating survivors and perpetrators soon became the focus of our research as we turned to explore the process of how the lesbian community in Chicago has understood, confronted, and responded to domestic violence.

Purpose Statement

The purpose of this study is to explore the lesbian community's response to domestic violence by drawing on the experiences and perspectives of mental health professionals who have expertise in domestic violence and work predominantly with lesbians in domestically violent relationships. By focusing the present research on a community's process of addressing domestic violence, the researchers hope to expand on the existing domestic violence theories including psychological, psychosocial, sociocultural, feminist, and more recently, biopsychosocial models, and to enable those who work in the domestic violence field to examine and enhance services for lesbian survivors and perpetrators. The study was conducted within a feminist framework to elucidate providers' diverse experiences within the context of domestic violence. The feminist framework works from the following assumptions: gender, like race, class, age, and sexual orientation, is socially constructed; women have diverse lives and experiences; and the acknowledgment of diversity can help researchers avoid universalizing and stereotyping women's experiences; and women's narratives are a viable means to understanding women and giving voice to women's experiences.

METHODS

Sampling Procedures and Participants

The sampling strategies were purposeful and criterion-based. Participants were recruited through announcements, flyers and letters to professionals asking for volunteers. Participation was on a strictly voluntary basis.

Research participants were 15 professionals working in the field of lesbian domestic violence. Participants' ages ranged from 27 to 56. Two participants identified themselves as African-American, one as Latino, one Native-American, one as African-American/Native American and 10 identified as Caucasian. Two participants were male while 13 were female. Nine participants identified themselves as lesbian, one as bisexual, one as gay, and four identified as heterosexual. Participants' educational levels ranged from a high school degree with some college to having a doctorate in psychology.

Four participants had their own private practice while 11 worked for various agencies, inside and outside of the city of Chicago, that provided domestic violence services to a wide range of clientele across gender, race, and sexual orientation. All participants had experience working with lesbian domestic violence ranging from two to 10 years of experience. The majority of the participants also had experience working with heterosexual domestic violence, treating both survivors and perpetrators. Three participants also identified themselves as survivors of domestically violent relationships. In addition, several participants acknowledged their active involvement in the LGBT and domestic violence communities.

The overall population of Chicago, not only gay men and lesbian women, is diverse across race and ethnicity and consists of 41% Caucasian/White, 37% African American/Black, 26% Hispanic/Latino, and 4.5% Asian (U.S. Census, 2000). The gay and lesbian community has a strong history in Chicago including well-established neighborhoods, inroads into local and state politics, and community involvement and activism, such as the gay/lesbian pride parade that debuted in 1970.

Data Collection

Based on our interest in expanding domestic violence theory, we used a grounded theory method to analyze the data because its objective is to build theory that is faithful to and illuminates the area under study and that will hopefully have useful application. Although feminist researchers use a variety of qualitative styles, a shared premise of both feminist theory and research exists that women's reports of experience or the cultural products of their experience can be the focus of research. This focus on women's experiences can be transformative for participants, the researcher, and the broader social arena (Hall & Stevens, 1991).

The semi-structured face-to-face interviews lasted 45 to 60 minutes and consisted of 16 questions. The questions concerned identification of abuse, myths and misperceptions of abuse, and the impact of work on professionals. The questions focused on the following: (a) the lesbian community's current view and response to domestic violence, (b) the potential barriers to responding effectively, (c) the benefits to not responding and, (d) the elements required to change the current response.

The data consisted of more than 645 minutes of audio taped interviews with participants. The data was collected over a five-month period. The tapes were transcribed and field notes containing the first author's observations were collected during the interviews. All interviews were conducted by the first author for consistency purposes and so that the interviewer could be reflecting on themes that were emerging through the interviews. Nudist 4, a qualitative analysis program, was solely used to help enter, organize, and analyze the data.

Data Analysis

The analytic process was based on the grounded theory method (Strauss & Corbin, 1990). Data analysis began with open coding where sections of words, sentences, and phrases were examined for specific phenomena. The phenomena consisted of discrete events, happenings, and instances related to the lesbian community's response to domestic violence and the response of the survivors, perpetrators, and professionals. These segments were coded and the phenomena were conceptually labeled and developed into initial categories. The categories were further subdivided into subcategories. Each subcategory was measured on a continuum. These codes and categories were then systematically compared and contrasted against one another, producing more complex, abstract, and inclusive categories.

The data was then entered into the Nudist 4 program. An index tree display was used to organize the categories, their subcategories, and codes into a hierarchy. Analytic and self-reflective memos were written that consisted of the first author's thoughts, speculations concerning the data, and possible emerging theories about the lesbian community's response. These memos along with visual diagrams were then used as a basis for revising categories and mapping out the emerging theory and model.

Axial coding that involved making new connections between categories and subcategories followed open coding (Strauss & Corbin, 1990). As the categories were compared, questions were asked about how each category was related to the others in order to denote the nature of the relationships between them. A story line was then created to identify the core category and central phenomenon regarding the lesbian community's response to domestic violence. The story was laid out in graphic form to show a theoretical model of the central phenomenon (see results section). Saturation occurred at this stage.

The last step of analysis was "grounding the theory." Making and validating statements about the relationships between the central phenomenon and the other categories "grounded the theory." There were examples in the data that did not fit exactly but all cases were placed in the appropriate context to ensure the best theoretical fit. To address the area of researcher bias, cross-coding was conducted and feedback was elicited from other researchers to check for any inherent biases. Additionally, member checks with the participants were conducted to ensure that descriptions of the participants' stories were accurate.

FINDINGS

The analysis of the lesbian community's response to domestic violence produced the following theoretical model illustrated in Figure 1.

As the model illustrates, protecting the romantic ideal of the lesbian community and disunity were the causal conditions that led to the development of the phenomenon of lessening the load on the lesbian community. Participants viewed lessening as a set of actions taken by the Community in response to domestic violence. As participants discussed, the load itself was represented by three main components: (1) the stigma associated with domestic violence within a same-sex re-

FIGURE 1. Theoretical Model of the Lesbian Community's Response to Domestic Violence

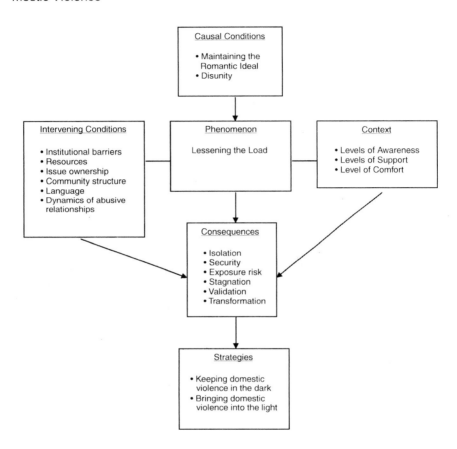

lationship, (2) the harmful effects domestic violence has on all of the members of the lesbian community, (3) the barriers faced by the lesbian community at large. The primary objectives of lessening the load are aimed at shielding the community from harm, reducing the burdens on the community and guaranteeing their survival. There are several actions the community adopts that effectively try to lessen the load which were discussed by participants along a continuum ranging from denial to identification and education. The consequences of those strategies resulted in a range of outcomes that were both costly and beneficial for the community. The context highlights the characteristics and background associated with the phenomena which included the levels of support, awareness and comfort in the lesbian community. The intervening conditions in the environment that influenced the phenomenon and impacted the strategies taken to lessen the load are institutional barriers, resources, issue ownership, community structure, language, and dynamics of abusive relationships. The strategies used to lessen the load are paradoxically keeping domestic violence in the dark and bringing domestic violence to light. The consequences resulting from those strategies are isolation, exposure risks, stagnation, security, validation, and transformation. The components of the model will now be discussed in more detail in the following sections.

Causal Conditions of Phenomena Related to Lessening the Load

Two types of causal conditions emerged from the data that gave rise to the phenomenon of lessening the load. The causal conditions were (a) protecting the romantic ideal of the lesbian community and (b) disunity. The majority of the participants discussed the efforts of the lesbian community to maintain its current identity as a romanticized, idealized, "utopian" existence.

The importance of maintaining the idealization of the community was viewed as a form of resistance. One participant remarked, "There are folks who resist knowing about domestic violence in the community because the idealization of the lesbian identity is important to some people." Another participant remarked on her own attempts to maintain the notion of a lesbian utopia:

> I think we, as a community, don't want to think of women as being abusive. I know when I first came out to myself, I thought of the whole lesbian utopia type of thing, where everything is going to be hunky dory and women, on the whole, are fair and wonderful. The reality is heterosexual people have the same problems that lesbians have. That was something that I figured out.

The lesbian community's romantic ideal was composed of the following categories: (a) maintaining the notion that women are non-violent, (b) community safety and, (c) close-knit connections. The belief that women are not capable of being violent towards each other, and that only men are violent, was a strong myth that many of the participants felt existed in the lesbian community. As lesbians and as women, it was difficult to acknowledge that women could be hurtful towards each other and go against the messages they learned growing up. As one participant explained:

> I think that women don't want to imagine other women hurting each other. There is something about someone of your own gender violating you. There is also a different message about boys fighting and girls fighting. I mean it's just not something girls do.

Acknowledging a woman's capacity for violence also challenged the professionals' sense of safety and immunity from harm in their community. One participant, who was a survivor of a domestically violent relationship, commented "(I'm) educated. I know about this stuff. How can I let this happen to me? I'm not immune to it." Another participant expressed her disbelief concerning the capacity for female violence and the "myth" of safety in the lesbian community.

> Even if you're in the community and not necessarily in a violent relationship or an abusive relationship, you still are in kind of a denial because that's how you're socialized. A person living in denial is a strong thing.

The lesbian community's closely-knit connections, where relationships were viewed as supportive and understanding, emerged as another component of the romantic ideal. One participant noted this component as the following:

> we (women) are all Kumbayah. We're a sisterhood. No one would ever hurt another woman. We would always support one another. These are my girlfriends and that's how we are socialized in a greater society.

Some participants felt that the close-knit connections in the community created conditions for isolation and protection from others. A participant described an element of the lesbian community as follows:

> They want to show the man as the perpetrator because we're all in this sisterhood. The women are in the sisterhood, and lesbian women and same-sex women are in (an) even deeper sisterhood . . . when really what started the sisterhood was the isolation.

The *second causal condition consisted of the disunity* within the lesbian community. Participants discussed how community diversity and community debates made it difficult for the community to have a unified understanding and response to domestic violence. The participants discussed diversity within the lesbian community across a wide range of variables that included race, ethnicity, socioeconomic status, political activism, and butch/femme roles. When asked to categorize how the lesbian community viewed domestic violence, participants responded:

> It depends on whom you are asking in the lesbian community because there's a big difference depending on which racial group, which ethnic group; even among lesbian activists, there are differences in the way they all talk about same-sex domestic violence and domestic violence in the heterosexual community.

Participants also remarked on how the community's diversity led to conditions where sectors of the lesbian community were isolated from each other.

Many of the participants also discussed location as it related to both survivors' and perpetrators' ability to access services in their communities. Certain areas of Chicago and the near suburbs were viewed as more saturated with services, including the North side of Chicago and the Northwest suburbs such as Oak Park. In areas where fewer lesbians lived, there was often a dearth of services and a multitude of individuals in need of assistance.

The *second category to emerge about community disunity was community debates*. Rather than having a unified viewpoint on domestic violence, participants explained that the community had varying perspectives that often resulted in community debates over the following: (a) how to define domestic violence and what qualified as domestic violence for an individual or a larger sector of the community and (b) how to treat survivors and perpetrators of domestic violence. One participant acknowledged that the varying perspectives on what constitutes domestic violence had existed over several years. She stated:

> I live in the suburbs now. I don't come into the city much. I'm not in the community like I once was ten years ago when we were having group forums at the coffee house. We started out talking about the problem of domestic violence. We had issues of people wanting to talk about them and us. Some people were saying it was a

feeling of psychodrama. Other people in that camp said it was a form of abuse.

Another participant remarked on the differences in perspectives across sectors of the community in terms of cultural norms:

> There's a pretty hardcore butch-femme lesbian community in which violence is just part and parcel it's normal and just to call it domestic violence is a shock. There's a lot of lesbians out there who think that pushing, shoving, slapping, and non-heavy duty physical violence are perfectly legitimate, just like there is a lot of straight folks who think it's perfectly okay. This is just what happens.

One participant who was an African-American lesbian also commented on the differences in perspectives across racial sectors of the community regarding cultural stereotypes:

> Some women don't identify it as being abusive; the African-American lesbian might say, "Well, you know, I have to deal with the problem because that's just how we act. We're just rough like that."

Despite the debate within the community about what constituted domestic violence, almost all of the participants defined domestic violence similarly and defined abusive behavior to include both physical and emotional abuse. The dynamics of the abuse concerned power and control over another person.

> I define abuse as a pattern of controlling behaviors that include psychological, physical, sexual, and economic coercion. A behavior that the goal is to manipulate people or dominate somebody else's feelings and behaviors, and it is to the detriment of somebody else, whether it's emotional or psychological, or physical, I think that's abusive.

However, participants discussed the debate about whether individual therapy or group therapy treatment approaches were more effective for victims and perpetrators. Moreover, many participants identified substance abuse as a common condition and a "competing issue" that professionals had to manage in their clinical work. Participants discussed the existence of conflicting views among service providers over which issue to treat first, the domestic abuse or the substance abuse, and the possibility of treating both problems simultaneously.

Context of Lessening the Load

The phenomenon of lessening the load was examined in the context in which the response was developed and maintained. Particular contextual markers were identified that related to both the causal conditions and the resultant phenomenon as well as influenced the strategies used to carry out the response. The contextual markers included: (a) levels of awareness, (b) levels of support and (c) levels of comfort.

Levels of Awareness

Levels of awareness refer to the knowledge that domestic violence occurs in the lesbian community and to what extent it occurs in same-sex abusive relationships. Awareness among the community ranged from low to high. The low end reflects minimal acknowledgement to outright denial that domestic violence exists in the lesbian community. Awareness was often lower for non-members of the lesbian community. For example, one participant discussed how the domestic violence movement in the heterosexual community was not prepared to acknowledge violence between two women. Another participant described awareness among providers:

> I think that there is still a significant amount of lack of understanding of same-sex relationships and controversy among therapists in not knowing how to work with them and treat them as normal human beings.

Levels of awareness varied depending on whether an individual or group was a member of the lesbian community. One participant describes awareness among members of the lesbian community as being higher:

> The people I'm generally around are activists and they tend to have an awareness of it, and have a lot of education about domestic violence including people I know at Horizons. I even know some bar owners who are aware and know what to do if it happens.

Awareness was often lower for non-members of the lesbian community. For example, one participant discussed how the domestic violence movement in the heterosexual community was not prepared to acknowledge violence between two women:

> A lot of the domestic violence movement holds, as its foundation, that the male is the perpetrator and the female is the victim. We are going to teach you about domestic violence and we're going to teach you about how to keep yourself safe. Keep yourself safe within your relationships, with your boyfriends, with your husbands, with your brothers, with your friends who are coming into the house, so that opens you up to not being prepared for domestic violence to come from another woman.

Awareness also varied among the individuals whose lives had been impacted by domestic violence. For some, being personally involved or knowing someone in an abusive relationship heightened their awareness.

Level of Support in the Community

The second contextual marker was the level of support in the community. Support ranges from low to high and refers to the community's willingness and ability to provide support to both individuals involved in same-sex abusive relationships and the professionals who provide services. While participants spoke about the romantic ideal as one of sisterhood and seamless support, many of them explained the conditions for most survivors and perpetrators as being a low level of support:

> It affects lesbians differently because they don't necessarily know how supported they would be, whether it's in the court or in their church, or in the community. There is not the same support for them as there is for heterosexual women that come in seeking services.

Under these conditions, many survivors and perpetrators were unable to seek assistance from their friends, family, and support groups. Greater support for survivors and perpetrators was often found in treatment environments where professionals were highly versed in same-sex domestic violence. All the participants commented that the availability of services in the community was limited and that this resulted in less support for women in same-sex abusive relationships. One factor cited for the limited services was minimal financial resources for both individuals seeking services and provider compensation:

> Women still don't really earn what men earn and we often end up with custody of children. And half of the women who identify as lesbians in heterosexual marriages and are out of those marriages suffer some of the same things that heterosexual women do.

> Domestic violence programs get the least amount of money of all the social services programs, but domestic violence is an issue that a lot of women feel strongly about and are willing to take less pay.

Some of the participants also expressed their perceptions of more services being available for survivors than perpetrators. A participant who worked with male and female perpetrators states, "they (mental health agencies) are making the same mistake in my opinion, that the straight community did and they are making their services victim specific." Analysis also showed that one of the causal conditions, the community's disunity, interacted with the amount of support provided to survivors and perpetrators as it was difficult to garner support across such a diverse group of individuals and perspectives.

Comfort Level

The third contextual marker was comfort level that ranged from low to high across survivors, perpetrators, and professionals. Under conditions of low comfort levels, both survivors and perpetrators were less likely to discuss the occurrence of domestic violence in their relationships with peers, family, and professionals. Participants attributed the discomfort to several factors including whether an individual was "out" about her sexual orientation, safety issues, and internalized negative feelings such as shame or guilt. One participant commented on her own difficulty in "coming out":

> You know we are already looked at sometimes by our parents and the people closest to us as being sinful or wrong or devious. How can we then tell them that we are in a situation with domestic violence? It was so hard for me to tell my parents that I was in this same-sex relationship. My God, you know, they are really struggling with that. I can't go back and tell them now that this person is

beating me up or emotionally abusing me and destroying me everyday. What am I going to tell them?

. Another participant commented on the impact of culture and location on comfort for individuals seeking services:

I think it is about a cultural barrier and a class barrier. A Latino might not want to go to a White provider. Somebody visiting on the South Side may not want to go to Howard Brown's provider or even downtown for services because they live too far away. Maybe it's too hard to get to. Maybe they don't feel comfortable leaving that neighborhood. Maybe they are not physically able to do so.

Many participants specifically highlighted the discomfort of the shelter environments for lesbian survivors. For example, one participant stated that lesbians are ostracized. "They can't even be in the shelters because it's more dangerous. Their partner can come in because they're a woman and they can just lie and be in the shelter, while the professionals in the shelter are thinking how great this is that we're protecting this other person." Participants concluded that there are a lack of shelters that are culturally sensitive to lesbians. On the opposite side, participants also spoke about the professionals' comfort level providing services to individuals in same-sex abusive relationships. Some participants voiced their own discomfort as well as recognizing their own limitations.

Intervening Conditions Influencing Communities Response to Domestic Violence

In addition to context, there were also intervening conditions that influenced the phenomenon of lessening the load. Six intervening conditions were identified: (a) institutional barriers, (b) resources, (c) issue ownership, (d) language, (e) community structure, and (f) abuse dynamics.

Institutional barriers. Institutional "barriers" refer to the powerful conditions and established societal structures that influence the community's response to domestic violence. The most salient barriers that emerged from the data were: (a) societal messages, (b) minimal systemic support, (c) and oppression. Several participants cited homophobia, both external and internal, as forceful societal messages that permeated the lesbian community. Many of them commented on the ingrained messages resulting from homophobic beliefs and their effects on the response of lesbian survivors. As well as playing a role in the reluctance of lesbian survivors to seek help, participants cited homophobia as steering the controversies in the shelter system and restricting the ability of shelter workers, many of whom are lesbian, to reach out to lesbian survivors. Some participants remarked on the high rate of homophobia and lack of acceptance of lesbians in the African-American, Latino, and Native American communities. Participants also commented on the daily messages that women in general, as well as lesbians, received from the media, religion, and their own families that devalued their gender and sexual orientation. Participants believed these societal messages, along with cultural differences and individual past experiences, had an overwhelming impact on lesbians involved in same-sex abusive relationships; as one participant described:

> First we have the homophobia the world puts on us. Then we have the homophobia that we take in as our own. Then we have our own shit from the past. Maybe we've been molested. Maybe a parent or a caretaker mistreated us. Maybe there are abandonment issues. So you take that person who may or may not be out for whatever reason and they are in a relationship with someone who is supposed to love them and nurture them unconditionally and they clearly aren't. The impact is devastating.

A common theme was that political, legal, religious, and media systems offered minimal support and gave little attention to the lesbian community and to the issue of domestic violence, and were biased towards the community. Participants discussed local as well as state and federal systems. Many participants expressed outrage and frustration at the lack of systemic support. For example:

> . . . political or legal protection, I mean in some states, if you call to report an abuse, you're going to be arrested for being gay . . . if you work for the police department in Chicago or Con Ed or certain major companies, you could lose your job.

> When you have a press conference to announce the numbers of domestic violence in the queer community and nobody from the (press community) shows, that's a clear message that we don't

care about this issue. It's not hot, it's not sexy like hate crimes, that's sexy and that's what people want to promote.

We can't get married, how screwed up of a message is that from our country to tell our community you cannot get married, I mean that is a perfect way to say you do not matter.

Politically, it might be easier to get money to cure lesbianism than to get money to support battered lesbians. There is still that religious stronghold that takes a stand against homosexuality.

Many of the participants viewed the members of the lesbian community as an oppressed group across several variables including gender, sexual orientation, race, and socioeconomic status. Some participants used the words "triple minority," "marginalized," and "devalued" when describing the oppression that lesbians faced both inside and outside of the their community. Most participants felt that being an oppressed group added to the load for individuals in same-sex abusive relationships and limited their abilities to respond. One participant shared the more optimistic view that being members of an oppressed group helped bring lesbians closer together in "bringing domestic violence to the forefront of the LGBT community."

Overall, many of the participants voiced strong feelings about the constraining effects of these "barriers" on the community, especially for those seeking support and acceptance as this participant described in the following statement:

I think, first off, that internal and external homophobia can lead to the feeling that they are huge failures. Being taught your whole life that being gay is not okay, not healthy, not a viable option and then becoming an adult who is battered by somebody who is a lesbian, it just compounds your own self to see resources working against you. For instance, you might call CPD (Chicago Police Department) and you get different treatment than a straight couple, and of course you're not going to get services or get into the shelter or tell your friends that it's happening because you're sick for being gay and on top of that you are in a violent relationship but people blame you for being a victim of violence which really compound(s) people's silence.

Resources. Overall, most of the participants spoke about the minimal financial resources available to the lesbian community. Limited resources were a primary condition that affected the community's process of responding to domestic violence. When asked about barriers in the community, one participant touted the importance of money when she stated, "there are other barriers, but money would address so many of them." Some participants commented on both the allocation and competition for resources, within and outside of the lesbian community, as intervening with how much the community had available to them.

Issue ownership. This category refers to existing debates regarding who is responsible for addressing domestic violence in the lesbian community. Participants perceived these debates to occur between the lesbian community and two overlapping groups: (a) the heterosexual domestic violence community, and (b) the battered women's movement, which included members of both lesbian and heterosexual orientations. One participant described the issue of ownership of addressing domestic violence as one of fear among heterosexual members of the battered women's movement:

> There is a great fear, if you lose control over the issue of domestic violence, are straight women going to get the attention they need if gay women and gay men are getting the attention. Will people forget about straight women?

Participants discussed their own varying perspectives as to who has been leading and who should be at the helm of responding to domestic violence. One participant stated, "I think that the domestic violence community needs to address the issues better and not just leave it to the lesbians and bisexuals in the community to do their work." One participant called for lesbians to hold more leadership positions in the community in regards to addressing domestic violence because "the lesbian community has to work against homophobia, while the straight community didn't have to work against heterosexuality." Several participants acknowledged the pioneering efforts of lesbians in the battered women's movement to address domestic violence between men and women. Participants also remarked on the external and internal conflict for lesbians involved in the movement to change their focus from men who batter women to women battering other women. This factor added heat to the debates over ownership.

Language. This condition specifically referred to the following; (a) how and by whom domestic violence had been verbally labeled and visually presented to the lesbian community and, (b) the labels attached to those involved in domestically violent relationships. Some of the participants remarked on the dominant use of "heterosexual language" versus "gender neutral language" inside and outside of the domestic violence community. Heterosexual language referred to language that focused solely on the violence between men and women. Several participants perceived this standard to be representative of the lack of sensitivity to lesbians in same-sex abusive relationships as well as a probable deterrent to seeking support and services.

Other participants spoke about the evolution of particular labels such as "victim," "batterer," "survivor," and "perpetrator" traditionally used to describe those involved in domestically violent relationships. Participants reacted to the manner in which these labels often categorized and potentially stigmatized individuals. One participant described the current climate in the domestic violence field as:

> I think the language that we use in this field makes it hard for people to access services. If we could somehow change it in some way I think that the doors would be more opened for people, but there's a stigma to be a victim, I don't want to be a victim, I think it might even be more of a stigma to be a victim than a perpetrator because our society is full of oppressors.

Some participants also discussed the weight of these terms and hypothesized about whether professionals should call abuse what it is or lighten and soften the terms they used with their clients with the hopes of less stigma and more lesbians seeking help from providers.

Community structure. The fifth intervening variable was community structure which refers to the community size and its boundaries. All of the participants acknowledged the blurred boundaries that existed in the community. The blurred boundaries resulted in the majority of members knowing each other, either professionally or personally. Many commented on their own experiences providing clinical services, both for survivors and perpetrators, in such a small community. These experiences reflected some of the challenges they faced as both members of the community and service providers, as these participants described:

> It seems to me like the biggest thing from my experience has been the fact that I always see my clients in the community.

> The community's small size makes it hard to be part of the community sometimes, because the victims tell what's happened to them, and to work in the community and have someone who is in treatment starting to date somebody who you know has perpetrated in the past, that part is always very difficult.

In addition to having contact with their clients outside of the therapeutic relationship, participants even remarked on working with their clients' abusers on committees or seeing them at social functions. For most participants, the blurred boundaries in the community led to feelings of discomfort and concerns about their safety. Many of them also discussed how the structure of the lesbian community created an environment that was less conducive for confidential, safe, and comfortable access to support and services for survivors and perpetrators.

Dynamics of abusive relationships. The last intervening condition was the dynamics of abusive relationships. Participants defined these dynamics as power and control. These dynamics were specifically evidenced in the strategies used to carry out the response of lessening the load. Participants noted that issues of power and control were not exclusive to relationships where domestic violence is present. Rather, participants discussed how these dynamics are active in all relationships because we are all exposed to the same messages and models about how we gain power and use it to manipulate and control others. Participants discussed the fluctuation of power in relationships and how the normalization of these differences was influential for survivors. For example, one participant said, "over a period of time, the victim starts to believe that it's normal, and they believe that it is not bad."

In addition to the norms about power and control in relationships, participants described that dynamics of abusive relationships acted to either facilitate or constrain the strategies used by the community to handle, manage, and carry out the phenomenon of lessening the load. While participants expressed that survivors could often tolerate the abuse for a period of time, eventually, the dynamics were seen to inhibit a survivor's response. One participant discussed:

> A person can take the emotional abuse without fighting back, only for so long, without it actually affecting them as a person, and finally they become more and more insecure. They begin to not believe in themselves, not to stand up for themselves, and the more that the person with the power uses her power, then the more destructive that is to the abused.

Participants discussed that because the perpetrators' behavior was justified by the norms and messages in society, this acted to facilitate their response in which they continued to abuse their partners and lessen their load.

Strategies for Lessening the Load in the Community

In the presence of the context and intervening conditions described above, the community employed the strategies necessary to lessen the load on each other as well as themselves. Two core groups of strategies emerged for lessening the load: (a) keeping domestic violence in the dark and (b) bringing domestic violence to light. The lesbian community at large, the survivors, and the perpetrators used the first core group of strategies. Strategies used to keep domestic violence in the dark included; (a) denial, (b) silence, (c) minimization, (d) delegating responsibility to a small group, and (e) prioritizing.

Denial. Almost all of the participants commented on the denial employed by some members of the lesbian community to keep domestic violence in the dark. One participant remarked on the long tradition of using denial when she stated:

> From all the women that I have seen, it is a great denial. The denial that I've seen in the gay and lesbian community is the same denial that I've seen for the past 25 years about domestic violence within the family context.

Participants also viewed some of the behaviors of survivors and perpetrators as evidence of their use of denial in their abusive relationships.

Silence. As an alternative strategy to denying that domestic violence existed, participants felt that parts of the community had chosen to be silent and not discuss the issue, at home or in public. One participant remarked on the community's knowledge and silence:

> We're sisters. We're lesbians. We're standing together against men who are present and so we are not going to say that violence is within our community even though everybody knows someone. They know friends who are in it, or who have been in it. They have partners who were perpetrators or were victims in previous relationships.

Minimization. The third strategy, minimization, was carried out in the community by relabeling domestic violence as something else or relegating it to pertain only to physical abuse. Examples of relabeling included "mutual battery," "cat fights," and "self-defense." Participants viewed the re-labeling of domestic violence on the part of the community as actions to minimize the level and severity of abuse between two women as participants described:

> The myth is that it doesn't happen, the myths are that it is not serious, for men it's boys will be boys and for women, it's catfights.

> When it is two women fighting, abuse could be occurring but people won't see it as abusive because the victim is also physical fighting back at some point.

> My experience is that lesbians have a tendency to minimize abuse and describe it as mutual combativeness which is basically where all the girls are on Viagra, and at the same time get into it or have an episode.

When defining domestic violence, participants also highlighted how the community only acknowledged physical abuse and minimized other forms of abuse including emotional, sexual, and financial.

Delegation of responsibility to small group. The fourth strategy to keep domestic violence in the dark was the delegation of responsibility to a small group. Many of the participants expressed that the overall task of addressing domestic violence and providing services had been put on the shoulders of a few by the lesbian community. Being among the small group of professionals who were providing services, many participants expressed strong feelings about shouldering the responsibility for the community. As one participant described his efforts of advertising domestic violence services in weekly gay and lesbian publications for over two years, he remarked that he had received only two referrals and stated emphatically, "what that tells me is that the leaders of the lesbian community do not see domestic violence as an issue."

Prioritizing. The last strategy, prioritizing, emerged in the voices of some participants as an effective tool that interfered with the community's ability to respond to the controversial and potentially stigmatizing issue of domestic violence. The action of prioritizing was seen by participants in two ways: (a) community focus on other pertinent and relevant issues and (b) protecting the lesbian culture from outside perceptions. Priorities cited by participants included the lesbian cancer health initiative, working towards human rights, and gender equality for women. Participants also discussed some of the priorities for the community as being focused on "just getting through the day."

Several participants discussed the community's efforts to protect the community from damaging perceptions including being viewed as "sick," "perverted," and "dysfunctional." Participants believed that these perceptions were often the result of homophobic and heterosexist beliefs in the dominant culture. Participants also highlighted the community's priority to enhance the image of the lesbian community rather than air the community's "dirty laundry" by acknowledging domestic violence in lesbian relationships. One participant described the act of prioritizing in the lesbian community in the following statement:

> We are not all perfect, and when you have to try to get recognition and put your best self forward, you don't want to give out anybody any kind of chink in the armor by starting to talk about violence.

Participants, as voices for the professional community who worked in the field of lesbian domestic violence, used the second group of core strategies to bring domestic violence to light. These strategies included: (a) identification, (b) dismantling beliefs, (c) outreach, (d) holding others accountable, (e) collaboration, (f) bridging experiences, and (g) self-care. All participants discussed their own methods of identifying abuse when working with women in same-sex relationships. Some participants used more formalized methods such as structured interviews where others used their "gut" reactions.

Identification. Some participants emphasized the importance of training to aid in accurate identification and distinguishing violence in same-sex relationships versus heterosexual relationships. The act of distinguishing abuse was considered to be an integral and challenging part of identification. Participants commented on their own strategies to distinguish between survivors and perpetrators including looking for helpful clues in how both partners in a same-sex abusive relationship presented during an intake or a therapy session. One participant described isolation as one sign she looked for in addition to these others:

> I look for isolation. Typically the survivor is the one who is extremely isolated. I look for financial aspects such as who controls the credit cards, the check books, or the checking account, all the way to sex and who instigates sex, and how does the sex go. Are

you made to do things you really don't want to do, do you get the orgasm or does your partner. What's dinner time like?

Participants also commented on the common occurrence of individuals identifying themselves as both a survivor and perpetrator and the added challenges this raised for identification and treatment.

Dismantling beliefs. The second strategy, dismantling beliefs, referred to the participants' attempts and directives to challenge existing assumptions about the lesbian community, the individuals in same-sex abusive relationships, and their own preconceived notions concerning the issues at hand. One participant discussed her own attempts to challenge the denial about domestic violence in the community.

> If you're dealing with domestic violence, you need to learn about how it impacts lesbians, too, so you can better serve them and actually be resources for them, too, because if a lesbian goes into E.R. and they look around and see that there is a poster with a beat-up woman and a man in the background, that lesbian will know that this isn't the place for me because I'm not represented here. If they go to court and get laughed at as they are getting an order of protection, if their partner is a woman, they might drop the case. What we've tried to do is dismantle the system that says don't talk about this, and that it doesn't exist so shut up, and say it does happen.

Another participant discussed her own strategies for challenging survivors' beliefs about themselves:

> I talked to a woman; she was lesbian, who came from Michigan. I talked to her for a year and a half, and I would say to her to go to a shelter, and she told me, it's easy for you to say that, because you don't have to leave everything. I told her I think it takes a lot of courage to withstand such abuse, that, even at some point, when you are at the verge of losing your soul, how much more can you lose. We can always get another job, we can always get everything else, but when you lose your soul, that's the roots, the very essence of your life, when you lose that you got nothing, then you will be dead, you will be breathing, but you will be dead. She said the fear of losing her soul was key for her.

Among the many assumptions that participants challenged were gender-based stereotypes of lesbian women, a perpetrator's ability to heal, and the origins of abusive behavior. A participant remarked on the assumption of gender-based roles in lesbian relationships:

> One (assumption) is that the butch is always the abuser. My experiences are the opposite. I have found that the femme is more likely to be the abuser in the butch-femme relationship. I don't have any statistics to prove it, but the data has shown that because the femme generally has that privilege in a relationship and the butch doesn't, the butch often may have less resources.

Participants highlighted the importance of viewing domestic violence as gender neutral and acknowledging the range of human capabilities; as one participant explained:

> I don't think the notion of women being violent towards each other has been accepted. It is harder to accept that woman are actually dangerous and are capable of abuse.

While being interviewed, some participants exhibited openness about their efforts to examine their own beliefs about lesbians and themselves:

> I challenge my own beliefs and work on dismantling all the disbelief that I might have including homophobic beliefs.

> At one of my classes at the University, there were a number of women in one of my women studies classes. We had to do a project and then share it with someone who was different, and give each other feedback. I shared mine with a lesbian woman and she wrote "a heterosexual perspective" all over my paper. It was a wonderful experience that I had and it made me realize that I really have to look at my heterosexism, how I present to people, and educating myself further.

Outreach. Many of the participants spoke about existing outreach efforts in the lesbian community including their own efforts. Several of them acknowledged the need for increased community education and services for domestic violence.

> In the hospital E.R.s, the courts, and among police and social workers, there needs to be so much more education, holistic edu-

cation about LGBT sensitivity. I am a big proponent of our educational systems teaching our children about gays, straight, that it's all really the same, the same meaning equal, healthy and viable, because until that happens we will all be different.

We need more domestic violence services than we have, we need services for batterers, as well as batterees. We need our services thought through carefully by the agencies providing them, and a community psychology outreach function that would do discussions and psycho-educational things and stuff like that.

Some participants spoke about the lack of response to outreach efforts by the lesbian community:

I go to the Chicago Metropolitan Battered Women's Network, where we have a specific LGBT committee that meets regularly. I think that the efforts are there to reach out and I know that other agencies are making really huge attempts to reach out to the lesbian community but they're just not reaching back.

Some participants also highlighted the importance of increasing the amount of culturally-relevant services as well as cultural sensitivity among providers; as one participant explained:

We need more mainstream domestic violence providers to be more sensitive to lesbian issues. We need more education among mainstream providers, and their needs to be more choices on the South Side, more choices on the West Side, more choices in Oak Park. I think their needs to be more people of color doing LGBT work, more Spanish speakers, more African Americans, and more Asian persons.

In addition, participants highlighted the importance of increasing the amount of culturally relevant services, as well as cultural sensitivity among providers.

Holding others accountable. The fourth strategy of holding others accountable refers to the lack of accountability of the perpetrators. Participants emphasized the reluctance of both professionals and the community at large to hold perpetrators accountable for their actions. Participants viewed accountability as a necessary strategy to bring domestic violence into the light. Many participants touted the belief that when perpetrators are not held accountable for their abusive behavior, the chances are small that they will either name or change their behavior.

Participants also discussed how holding other women accountable was inconsistent with the feminist ideals about equality and support for all. Participants spoke about the struggle and debate for women to hold each other accountable when they are both the oppressor and the oppressed. One participant explained:

> It's different than holding men accountable. Women need to be handled more delicately. They need to be held accountable for being a perpetrator but we also have to recognize their "victim stance" and understand where power comes from and how it works.

Collaboration among professionals. Collaboration among professionals was the fifth strategy participants discussed to produce a more unified and integrated approach to domestic violence both inside and outside of the lesbian community. One participant spoke about her own attempts to integrate lesbian perpetrators into her program that had primarily treated heterosexual perpetrators:

> I know I'm violating some of the norms out there about what you should do and not do, but at the same time, a woman wanted the services. She was told at any point she could drop out if the group did not feel right. We could do something on a more individual basis.

Bridging experiences. Alongside collaboration, bridging experiences emerged as the sixth strategy. This strategy referred to creating safe environments where women could come together to share their experiences of abuse including the powerful therapeutic effect of groups. One participant described the therapeutic effect of groups, when individuals are brought together who share a common ground:

> To hear other women who have gone through that and have survived, and went to court and got laughed at or their parents said that you're gay, you're sick and you're being abused. To have the community around you to lift you up and say, this is not what you deserve, you can have better; I think women can gain from that.

There are so many social groups in Chicago for lesbians but there needs to be more.

Some participants also highlighted the importance of group safety in order to enhance group effectiveness as well as the integration of members of diverse experiences and backgrounds.

Self-Care. The seventh and final strategy referred to the participants' own personal strategies of self-care. These strategies were seen as necessary devices to ensure participants' own emotional and physical well-being while working in the field of lesbian domestic violence. Forms of self-care included consultation groups, exercise, and even an occasional massage.

Consequences of Strategies for Lessening the Load

The strategies used to both keep domestic violence in the dark and bring it to light were not without consequences. In some cases, the strategies resulted in negative consequences for the community including isolation, exposure risks, and stagnation. Almost all of the participants spoke about the isolation that members of the lesbian community experienced, including individuals involved in same-sex abusive relationships. Isolation refers to limited choices and limited access to services. One participant described how participants felt their choices were limited both in and out of abusive relationships:

> They are fearful and they can't step out and say it is happening so that isolates them more. If they are out of the relationship, they are still isolated because they can't talk about it and it's a small community too.

Participants also expressed how being isolated from services might lead some to search for assistance "underground" rather than being able to access help in their community.

All participants mentioned exposure risks as a potentially costly outcome of actively responding to the issue of domestic violence. Risks for the community ranged from the airing of their "dirty laundry" to the greater society, to individuals "being outed" to their family, friends, and co-workers. Participants described how these risks could potentially result in negative publicity that could increase discrimination against the lesbian community, as well as the alienation from family, friends, and the loss of jobs.

Issues of safety were seen as risks for both individuals involved in same-sex abusive relationships and professionals working in the field of domestic violence. One participant noted that many of her clients who were survivors "could never feel safe in their surroundings," even after the abuse had ended and/or they had left the abusive relationship. Other participants explained exposure and safety risks for survivors in these terms:

> The whole thing is about being visible. Once you become visible, people are going to know that you are the woman who is being abused.

> One real fear factor is that if (survivors) come out about the abuse, they might be in serious danger, physical danger, and even economic danger.

Participants described how being exposed to those involved in same-sex abusive relationships often increased their level of fear and decreased their feelings of safety, both personally and professionally. Two participants described the results of their exposure:

> When working with my clients, I would get scared for them, and I would start thinking of what could happen when they leave me and go home. What if they got raped or get called a fat, lazy bitch. My mind just went with them when they walked out my door.

> I generally feel less safe and I am kind of protective of making sure people don't have my phone number. I watch when I'm outside or at home for anybody who is not supposed to be there because I hear lots of people say to me "my partner doesn't like you, because you're going to tell them to believe me."

Additionally, participants described health risks associated with exposure including panic attacks and depression.

Participants also discussed how exposure to domestic violence could sometimes result in people being more hyperaware and hypersensitive to the issue in the lesbian community. Participants even described themselves as being "overly cautious," "vigilant" and "paranoid," especially those participants who had been involved in a domestically violent relationship.

Stagnation, a lack of movement and change, was seen as a negative consequence of lessening the load. Participants highlighted that by keeping domestic violence in the dark, abusive behaviors and damaging beliefs would be perpetuated inside and outside the lesbian community and perpetrators would continue to "benefit from silence." Participants characterized the devastating effects of perpetual abuse on survivors:

> I would characterize the women I worked with as the walking wounded, not even really there, just empty carcasses, not knowing who they were, not knowing what was important to them anymore.

Participants also remarked on the stagnating response of the battered women's movement to domestic violence in the lesbian community. In regards to the overall lack of change over the past 20 years, one participant stated, "some people are still back in the 1980s" and continue to narrow their focus on "domestic violence in white heterosexual relationships." Another participant commented on how same-sex domestic violence was "only a footnote to heterosexual domestic violence and still in its infancy." Both of these perceptions illuminated a slow and arduous path to addressing domestic violence in the lesbian community.

Other strategies resulted in the hope for more positive consequences including security, validation, and transformation. Security referred to the following: (a) maintaining their romanticized identity of the community, (b) maintaining connections in the community and (c) maintaining stability and predictability.

> Domestic violence is discounted, it's ignored, and it's not talked about, because it is a blemish on the lesbian community that women are battering other women.

Participants remarked on the importance of maintaining connections, especially for survivors. One participant stated, "they have somebody in their life and even if it's costing them their self-worth, and self-respect, at least they're not alone."

Participants also discussed the benefits of using denial and silence for both survivors and perpetrators in maintaining stability and predictability. Two participants described these benefits:

> It's the same benefits for all of us who are in denial to stay in the fields like they're secure; even though you're hit and raped or hav-

ing money taken from you, you know that there's some stability in it because you know when to expect the next beating.

A person who is abusive can keep that covered up. They don't have to put it out there that they are doing this horrible thing because it is normalized.

Validation involved the processes of naming the violence, having your voice heard, and being recognized and accepted. One participant discussed the importance for lesbians to have the same opportunity as heterosexual women to speak out on domestic violence without having to deal with ridicule. She went on to describe her feelings when women are able to speak out:

I'm always really thrilled when a woman actually comes out and says that this has happened to me, because it's a freedom, a sign that she can't be silent anymore, and that she feels comfortable saying that to me.

Another participant remarked on the positive outcome of a group she headed where lesbian women, even professionals who had been survivors, came forward and were able to name the violence. Several participants acknowledged the "barriers" that lesbians faced as well as the need for them to be recognized and accepted by the dominant cultures. Two participants discussed some of these barriers and the need to break them down:

Any minority community struggles with getting recognition whether it's economic, political, or social. They still need to be heard, to be seen, and to be recognized, and to be taken seriously as a whole.

Many lesbians have learned their whole lives marriage is not an option and on top of that you can't have this ceremony. We need to break this shit apart so that when we get into a relationship, we've been taught that we are just as valuable, the relationship is just as valid, and you can talk about what is happening in it.

Transformation referred to the healing process for survivors and perpetrators and the push as well as hope for new ways to view domestic violence. Participants discussed the resiliency of survivors and the ability for perpetrators to change their behaviors. In discussing her work, a participant commented on the gratification of witnessing the feelings of "both victims," survivors and perpetrators, and healing because of the work that she does in the domestic violence field.

Participants highlighted the successful progress that the community had made in bringing domestic violence into the light:

> Five years ago, nobody wanted to talk about it because it didn't exist but it is definitely changing and there are more books about lesbians and domestic violence. There are a number of support groups that have been popping up and I definitely see the movement toward where people are saying let's talk about it.

Participants also remarked on how progress was being made in bringing cultural differences into the light and widening the scope of domestic violence. One participant remarked on the community's efforts including her own:

> Domestic violence is being treated differently now because I just worked on a campaign that is focusing on women of color including African-American and Latino women. We actually had a poster where there are two African-American women on the poster in Spanish that I loved. So I think, definitely think we are trying to break down some stereotypes.

Additionally, participants discussed how working in the field of lesbian domestic violence and their own experiences in abusive relationships had transformed them:

> It has given me more awareness, and made me more flexible to go in and out of every community to utilize what I know, and facilitate women's power by giving them the information and creating a space for them. They heal themselves. We are just the facilitators.

> From my experience, I've learned that I am not any worse than anyone else, and being a lesbian doesn't mean that I am never going to be violent or that I will always have the wonderful utopian experience. Learning that I am like everybody else has had a very stabilizing effect on my self-esteem.

Lastly, participants highlighted the need to " shake things up" by developing a broader understanding and new approaches to domestic violence. One participant spoke passionately as he described the need for a . "paradigm shift" in the field of domestic violence:

> The party line has always been that men have been trying to exercise power over women since the beginning of time and that the socialization process has been the major contributor to male violence against women. So why are women trying to exercise power over other women? My belief is that socialization is a piece of it but it's not the biggest part. It is really about the specific power and control issues for the person who is choosing to abuse. We are talking about issues including the psychological and emotional challenges each individual faces. After a convention, a woman said to me, I know what you are saying, but I just hate to see this happening to the domestic violence movement. I told her that all movements get to actual treatment and theory and that's where we are now including getting more done on domestic violence in the LGBT community.

Another participant described how women were beginning to feel empowered and undergo a transformation of their own:

> It is a depressive thought that women are perpetrating violence on each other because we have come so far, from where we couldn't even vote. I think it is pretty devastating but also motivating because women are saying no to violence in their community, talking about the issue, and attending our rallies and seminars. And they're saying I'm not going to live my life this way and I know that I am just as powerful as men. The big impact is that no one has to live or suffer in silence as our mothers did generations ago.

DISCUSSION

Parallels with Existing Research

The present research is congruent with the existing research on the lesbian community's response to domestic violence and the impact on those involved in same-sex abusive relationships. Throughout this study, participant's "voices" serve to confirm that the community's strategies of denial, minimization, and silence are consistent with the strategies that researchers have documented to be the primary response of the lesbian community since domestic violence was first addressed over 15 years ago (Lobel, 1986; Walber, 1988; Renzetti, 1992; Russo, 1992, 1999; Peterman & Dixon, 2003). Despite the outreach attempts noted by participants to increase awareness, acknowledgment, support, and comfort about domestic violence in the lesbian community, women involved in same-sex abusive relationships remain isolated, fearful, and reluctant to identify and seek help for the abuse. Families, friends, social networks, and non-mental health sectors of the lesbian community offer minimal support and participate in the violence through passive observance, minimizing, and rationalizing the abusive behavior of the perpetrators (Lobel, 1986; Lundy, 1994; Allen & Leventhal, 1999). Barriers including institutional sexism and homophobia continue to confront survivors, resulting in internalized hatred, shame, fear, and self-blame (Leeder, 1988; Pharr, 1990 as cited by Elliot, 1990; Allen & Leventhal, 1999). Lesbian lifestyles are often not supported by legal, political, or religious systems, therefore lesbian women do not have the same access to the basic human rights, freedoms, and protection that men and women in the dominant culture are afforded (Pharr, 1990 as cited by Elliot, 1990; Russo, 1992). Moreover, due to homophobia in the shelter system, shelters are often not comfortable or safe havens for survivors and shelter workers are not readily able to reach out to lesbian survivors (Irvine, 1984 as cited by Elliot, 1990; Walber, 1988; Pharr, 1990 as cited by Elliot, 1990). The community's small size and blurred boundaries add to the challenge of providing confidential, safe, and comfortable access to support and services for survivors and perpetrators.

The community's attempts and desire to protect and maintain the idealized vision of a supportive, safe, and non-violent lesbian image remain active. Maintaining the idealized image results in continued avoidance rather than acknowledging a female capacity for violence for all women (Irvine, 1994).The community's efforts to uphold this "utopian" existence have also been part of a process of promoting the illusion of what lesbianism should be instead of recognizing the realities within the community (Enos & Rollins, 1988 as cited by Elliot, 1990; Russo, 1992; Allen & Leventhal, 1999).

The participants' own strategies of working to increase awareness, support, and acknowledgement about lesbian domestic violence are consistent with the strategies suggested by researchers and activists (Enos & Rollins, 1988 as cited by Elliot, 1990; Pharr, 1990 as cited by

Elliot, 1990; Russo, 1992, 1999; Allen & Leventhal, 1990). Areas of improvement and growth for the community include increasing validation and acceptance for survivors, a therapeutic healing process for survivors and perpetrators, and shifting current ways of theoretically understanding and viewing domestic violence to incorporate its effect on diverse groups beyond white heterosexuals.

The fact that this study showed significantly similar results when compared to the existing literature that addresses same-sex abusive relationships is not surprising, but this striking similarity raises concerns regarding the community's stagnant response. Both existing research and the results of this study reflect minimal changes in the lesbian community's response to domestic violence across the last 15 years. Both the participants and lesbian domestic violence researchers (Renzetti, 1992; Allen & Leventhal, 1999; Russo, 1992, 1999; Peterman & Dixon, 2003) emphasize the importance of taking a broader systemic and context-specific view when evaluating and understanding the community's response to domestic violence. Exploring and understanding the socio-political-cultural forces, including oppression, sexism, and homophobia and the dynamics of power and control that enable domestic violence to occur and be sustained in the current climate of the lesbian community, can help us understand how the community's response to domestic violence has been stagnant since lesbian battering was first addressed 15 years ago. Additionally, evaluating the similarities and differences between heterosexual and lesbian domestic violence as well as violence between women, is integral to both identifying and addressing abuse as well as the demand for equal services for battered lesbians and recognition and accountability on the part of domestic violence service providers.

Limitations

Threats to validity in qualitative work generally result from errors in description or interpretation (Maxwell, 1998). The descriptions in this study are based on the first author's observations, recorded in detailed notes, and complete transcripts of audio taped interviews. As previously stated, sampling for this study was purposeful as the participants were selected based on their ability to be uniquely informative in the area of lesbian domestic violence as well as being representative of different sectors of both the lesbian and heterosexual community across race, ethnicity, gender, and sexual orientation. Consequently, the results of this study are specific to this group and geographic setting (Chicago) and may not be externally generalized to other professionals or lesbian communities.

Implications

One participant explained the community's progress and movement towards social change for addressing lesbian domestic violence by stating, "we're 40 billion years behind the straight community and are taking baby steps and yet we are getting there . . . it's a long, long path to be on." The path this community is traversing has left us with two questions: (a) what are the necessary conditions for change to occur in order to "lessen the load" on the community and (b) how do we move from discourse towards agency while understanding the shaping power of the social context?

A useful model to explore change is the transtheoretical approach to the "processes of change" proposed and applied by Prochaska, Norcross, and DiClemente (1994). In this model, proposed stages of change for individuals are discussed as a series of steps that "spiral" upward and lead to individuals making successful changes. This model has been primarily applied to individual specific behaviors such as smoking, overeating, depression, and physical abuse. It may be useful to evaluate the stages reflected by the community response. The stages are as follows: pre-contemplation, contemplation, preparation, action, maintenance, and termination (Prochaska, Norcross, & DiClemente, 1994). While all of the stages are built upon one another, the stages that are reflective of the community's response: pre-contemplation, contemplation, preparation, and action can be considered.

Although there are a small number of individuals and groups in the lesbian community who fluctuate between the preparation and action stages, the majority of members in the community are primarily in the stages of pre-contemplation and contemplation. Oppressive forces, including sexism, homophobia, and the community's propensity to avoid conflict in favor of self-preservation, act together to isolate and trap the community in these stages.

The model proposed by Prochaska and colleagues (1994) highlights the importance of the following processes to transition out of the pre-contemplative and contemplative stages, towards preparation and action: consciousness-raising, self-evaluation, and social liberation. These processes have had, and can continue to have, important implications for the manner in which the community can work to bring about internal change and move towards greater agency. Consciousness-raising refers to heightening internal and external awareness about a problem through the use of accurate and truthful information (Prochaska et al., 1994). Consciousness-raising continues to be a critical process for the community to increase insight, understanding, and identification of domestic violence.

The process of self-evaluation involves evaluating one's identity before and foreseeing one's identity after the problem is solved, and reconciling the problem with one's personal values (Prochaska et al., 1994). The process of self-evaluation will be focused on the goal of integration and calls for the community to redefine the lesbian identity. Social liberation entails a process of altering the social environment in ways that can help others change themselves (Prochaska et al., 1994). The current social environment in the community is one of denial, disunity, disempowerment, and fear. Altering the environment involves breaking down the denial and finding new, safer ways to address conflict that do not lead to further oppression, abuse, and divisiveness among the members of the lesbian community.

Prochaska and his colleagues (1994) identify several broad strategies and specific techniques to shift resistance and to move towards the action phase. The current participants and previous researchers describe similar broad strategies and techniques. They include confronting the defense mechanisms of denial, minimization, and rationalization. They also include advocacy and policy interventions, increasing education, emphasizing supportive relationships and creating safe environments in which to seek those relationships.

When considering treatment options for domestic violence, it would be useful to evaluate the stages that those involved in domestically violent relationships are in, because treatment paradigms may be more effective with individuals in one stage and less effective with individuals in another stage. Identifying the stages via assessment, targeting the dimensions of each stage of change has the added benefit of identifying the appropriate mode of service delivery (i.e., individual versus group therapy). In addition, if women are seen as "knowers" and "experts" concerning their own experiences, then looking to survivors and perpetrators themselves for both answers and agency may be the remedy to developing more accessible and effective treatment.

Future Research

Some areas for future research might include the following: a systematic comparison of the perceptions of groups from varying positions in the social hierarchy concerning the dynamics of abusive relationships, and what maintains abuse in their communities, examining how providers' specific social positions influence their own awareness and sensitivity of women's diverse experiences of domestic violence; an exploration of whether the present definitions and labels have been beneficial for women involved in same-sex abusive relationships; and an evaluation of the efficacy of current treatment paradigms, identifying the gaps and how they can best be addressed by professionals.

REFERENCES

Allen, C., & Leventhal, B. (1999). History, culture, and identity: What makes GLBT battering different. In B. Leventhal & S. Lundy (Eds.), *Same-sex domestic violence: Strategies for change* (p. 73-83).Thousand Oaks, CA: Sage.

Bloom, R. L. (1998).*Under the sign of hope: Feminist methodology and narrative interpretation*. Albany, NY: State University of New York Press.

Brand, P. A., & Kidd, A. H. (1986). Frequency of physical aggression in heterosexual and female homosexual dyads. *Psychological Reports, 59*, 1307-1313.

Coleman, V. E. (1991). Violence between lesbian couples: A between groups comparison. Unpublished doctoral dissertation. California School of Professional Psychology, Los Angeles.

Crenshaw, K. W. (1994). Mapping the margins: Intersectionality, identity politics, and violence against women of color. In M. A. Fineman & R. Mykitiuk (Eds.), *The public nature of private violence* (pp. 93-118). New York: Routledge.

Davidson, T. (1978). *Conjugal crime: Understanding and changing wife beating pattern*. New York: Hawthorn.

Elliot, P. (1990.) *Confronting lesbian battering: A manual for the battered women's movement*. St. Paul, MN: Minnesota Coalition for Battered Women.

Fortunata, B., & Kohn, C. (2003). Demographic, psychosocial, and personality characteristics of lesbian batterers. *Violence & Victims, 18*(5), 557-568.

Frieze, I. H., & Browne, A. (1987). *Violence in marriage., Unpublished manuscript*.

Kelly, C. E., & Washarfsky, L. (1987). *Partner abuse in gay male and lesbian couples*. Unpublished manuscript.

Leeder, E. (1988). Enmeshed in pain: Counseling the lesbian battering couple. *Women & Therapy, 7*(1), 81-99.

Lobel, K. (1986). *Naming the violence: Speaking out about lesbian battering*. Washington: Seal Press.

Lundy, S. (1994). Abuse that does not speak its name: Assisting victims of lesbian and gay domestic violence in Massachussets. *New England Law Review, 28*(2), 273-311.

Maxwell, J. (1998). Designing a qualitative study. In L. Bicman & D. Rog (Eds.), *Handbook of applied social research methods* (pp. 69-100). Thousand Oaks, CA: Sage.

Peterman, L., & Dixon, C. (2003). Domestic violence between same-sex partners: Implications for counselors. *Journal of Counseling and Development, 81*(1), 40-47.

Pharr, S. (1986). Two workshops on homophobia. In K. Lobel (Ed.), *Naming the violence: Speaking out about lesbian battering.* Washington: Seal Press.

· Prochaska, J. O., Norcross, J. C., & DiClemente, C. C. (1994). *Changing for good.* New York: Avon Books.

Renzetti, C. M. (1988). Violence in lesbian relationships: A preliminary analysis of causal factors. *Journal of Interpersonal Violence, 3*(4), 381-399.

Renzetti, C. M. (1989). Building a second closet: Third party responses to victims of lesbian partner abuse. *Family Relations, 38,* 157-163.

Renzetti, C. M. (1992). *Violent betrayal: Partner abuse in lesbian relationships.* Newbury Park, CA: Sage.

Russo, A. (1992). A battered lesbian fights for recognition. *Sojourner, 17*(9), 14-17.

Russo, A. (1999). Lesbians organizing against lesbian battering. In B. Leventhal & S. Lundy (Eds.), *Same-sex domestic violence: Strategies for change* (pp. 83-97). Thousand Oaks, CA: Sage.

Strauss, A., & Corbin, M. J. (1990). *Basics of qualitative research: Grounded theory procedures and techniques.* Newbury Park, CA: Sage.

United States Census Bureau (2000). *Chicago City, Illinois, statistics and demographics.* Washington, DC: Author.

Walber, E. (1988). Behind closed doors: Battering and abuse in the lesbian community. In M. Shernoff & W. Scott (Eds.), *The sourcebook of lesbian/gay healthcare* (pp. 250-256). Washington, DC: National Lesbian/Gay Foundation.

doi:10.1300/J086v18n01_05

A Feminist Perspective of Resilience in Lesbian Couples

Colleen M. Connolly

SUMMARY. Lesbian couples experience a tremendous amount of societal stressors; yet demonstrate great resilience in rebounding from adversity. This article explores the stressors of cultural oppression, the implications of gender role socialization, the maintenance and coordination of identity disclosure, and the review, renewal and creation of family. It then highlights ways that lesbian couples exhibit resilience in long-term relationships. This article applies a feminist family therapy perspective to the stressors and resilience shown by lesbian couples with the hope of expanding theoretical understanding, sharpening clinical skills, and increasing effective and ethical work with this population. doi:10.1300/J086v18n01_06 *[Article copies available for a fee from The Haworth Document Delivery Service: 1-800-HAWORTH. E-mail address: <docdelivery@haworthpress.com> Website: <http://www.HaworthPress.com> © 2006 by The Haworth Press, Inc. All rights reserved.]*

KEYWORDS. Lesbian couples, feminist couple therapy/counseling, resiliency, feminist family therapy, family of origin, identity, gender role, feminist research, qualitative research

INTRODUCTION

Feminist family therapy is an important force for working with lesbian couples and understanding the strength and resilience they demon-

[Haworth co-indexing entry note]: "A Feminist Perspective of Resilience in Lesbian Couples." Connolly, Colleen M. Co-published simultaneously in *Journal of Feminist Family Therapy* (The Haworth Press, Inc.) Vol. 18, No. 1/2, 2006, pp. 137-162; and: *Lesbian Families' Challenges and Means of Resiliency: Implications for Feminist Family Therapy* (ed: Anne M. Prouty Lyness) The Haworth Press, Inc., 2006, pp. 137-162. Single or multiple copies of this article are available for a fee from The Haworth Document Delivery Service [1-800-HAWORTH, 9:00 a.m. - 5:00 p.m. (EST). E-mail address: docdelivery@haworthpress.com].

strate. Several feminist processes underscore this contention. To begin with, feminist theory starts with women's lives and experiences as central, normal, and valuable; it reveals knowledge gaps in the previous dominant conceptualization of the middle-class, White, Protestant, heterosexual, and male perspective (Goodrich, Rampage, Ellman, & Halstead, 1988; Halstead, 2003). It also acknowledges the need to continually examine the principles within theories and practices for the presence of sexist and heterosexist underpinnings, as these processes are not only insidious, but also embedded in what we consider to be state-of-the-art psychotherapeutic theories (Halstead, 2003).

In addition, feminism recognizes and voices how differently men and women experience self, other, and life, i.e., the widely-articulated experience of men and the largely ignored or misrepresented experience of women (Goodrich et al., 1988).

> To experience oneself as male in this society is to experience privilege. To experience oneself as female in this society is to experience personal responsibility for relationships. . . . The feminist perspective elucidates not only the differences between the genders but the power of one over the other. (Goodrich et al., 1988, p. 7)

Furthermore, feminist family therapy attempts to reveal society's arrangement and stratification by sexual orientation, race, and class, in addition to gender (Haddock, Zimmerman, & MacPhee, 2000). Remaining sensitive to the various and interlocking forms of oppression (Brown, 1995) and sustaining the commitment to fight against the other types of oppression that intersect with sexism (Haddock et al., 2000) are pivotal to the process, as "racism, sexism, heterosexism, and classism impede all individuals' ability to engage and participate in growth-fostering relationships" (Jordan & Hartling, 2002, p. 53).

However, some challenges still remain. According to Seem (2001), feminist family therapy has "privileged heterosexual couples. 'The centrality of power draws feminist therapists' attention primarily to heterosexual relationships–especially marriage, as the relationship in which the culturally prescribed power inequities between men and women have their most pernicious effects' " (Rampage, 1998, p. 353; Seem, 2001, p. 29). As a result, therapists may retain dominant views about what health and pathology look like and inadvertently apply these principles in their clinical work with lesbian clients, who have distinct stressors, norms, and relational processes of resilience (Seem).

Confronting patriarchy and sexism is not easy; it is a project that requires endurance and attention not only to the diagnostic labeling or interventions cloaked in misogyny but also to the subtle language distinctions and small behavioral nuances (Rampage, 1996). Sexism has informed the making of all couple relationships, just as it has informed the making of theories (Rampage, 1995). Moreover, our knowledge base and clinical application have evolved under the shadow of heterosexism (Brown, 1991; Long, 1996), and unexamined heterosexism can harm lesbian clients just as unexamined racism can harm ethnic minorities (Long, 1996).

These issues punctuate the importance of continuing to confront these –*isms* and amplifying our understanding of power in lesbian relationships. As we work within a feminist model, power and gender issues are not marginal issues to be addressed only when clients raise them but are central to the therapeutic concerns and outcomes. "Gender and the gendering of power are not secondary mediating variables *affecting* life; they *construct* family life in the deepest sense" (Goldner, 1989, p. 56). If power issues are not addressed, then problems persist (Parker, 2003).

A dynamic of power exists in every system, and it is "vital that we are able to examine how power is attained, used, lost, and managed in every system" (Halstead, 2003, p. 49). Perhaps the distinction of power proposed by feminists (Goodrich, 1991; Rampage, 1995) provides a useful lens: that of the coercive *power over* another in contrast to *power to*, which is "more akin to personal authority, the ability to perform and produce, and the freedom to do so" (Rampage, 1995, p. 264).

Feminist therapists employ a rebalancing of power within the relationship (May, 2001; Rothberg & Ubell, 1987). With lesbian couples, therapists often approach the couple with the "hope and expectation of an equal power base; however, power struggles arise," and these struggles are often more covert than within different-sex couples. In order to redistribute power, one must break away from gender stereotypes, open options, and view roles as fluid (Rothberg & Ubell, 1987). This restructuring process includes allocating roles and functions based on interests, abilities, and personal choices rather than gender (May, 2001), processes that lesbian couples must constantly negotiate and manage in their lives.

Feminists also remain committed to rebalancing and redefining families (May, 2001). They work against the ideology that a "normal family" exists, because it inaccurately represents actual families and stigmatizes other forms of relationships (Goodrich et al., 1988; Halstead,

2003), such as lesbian couplings. The centrality of women, scrutiny of theories and practices for sexism and heterosexism, attention to multiple forms of oppression, and the unpacking and rebalancing of power in relationships bolster and support our work with women entering into, maintaining, and sustaining relationships amidst the untenable cultural stressors.

STRESSORS

All families experience stressors, but lesbian families experience an inordinate amount of them. Before reviewing those stressors unique to lesbian couples, it appears important to provide a framework to better understand both stress and stressors. According to Boss (1988), stressors are different from stress in that they produce an event so significant that it disturbs the status quo and provokes change. Stressors, such as disclosure to family of lesbian identity, can generate such an event. Many stressors are non-volutional, events that are not sought out but just happen. Chronic stressors emerge from social conditions, such as sexism, heterosexism, and oppression, and can disturb a couple's equilibrium over time. An inordinate amount of ambiguous stressors exists from these social conditions, and lesbian couples often struggle to overtly identify that a stressor exists, much less gather all of the facts or distinguish from which direction the stressors come. Ambiguous events outweigh clear-cut events and can lead to feelings of hypervigilance, as couples wait and wonder, never being quite sure when trouble might surface.

Stressor events can occur concurrently or in quick succession, leading to what Boss (1988) refers to as "stress pileup" (p. 46). This accumulation of stressors can increase the couple's vulnerability and jeopardize their ability to recover, putting the relationship more at risk. When experiencing multiple stressors, the couple may be unaware of the distress or unable to recognize how close they are to their individual and/or relational threshold. When unexpected, non-normative stressors occur, couples can be pushed to extremes of adaptation; capabilities might be depleted or couples might be tested and pushed to even higher levels of competence (Patterson, 2002b).

Lesbian couples show such remarkable resilience and longevity and thrive in spite of a context of oppression that I focused my dissertation on this topic (Connolly, 1999) in an effort to learn more about their "secrets to success" (Laird, 1993, p. 319). Ten long-term couples, together for 10 to 25 years and ranging from 34 to 60 years of age, participated in a qualitative study. The participants were almost exclusively White, middle- to upper-middle-class socioeconomic status, with education ranging from some college to doctorates. Access to this type of sample is more likely when seeking lesbian couples willing to disclose about their relationship to a middle-class, White researcher. However, it continues the trend of overrepresentation of the white lesbian experience (Morgan & Brown, 1991), as lesbians of color are rendered invisible in scholarly research of both women of color and of lesbians (Greene, 1994).

The couples spoke about strength, resilience, and longevity in the first interview, with a second interview used for clarification, confirmation, and expansion (Connolly, 2005). I purposefully created an in-depth, open-ended interview in an attempt to potentiate the "richest" qualitative data (Mathews & Paradise, 1988, p. 231), and I use additional data during the following exploration of stressors.

STRESSORS UNIQUE TO LESBIAN COUPLES

The literature often clusters the experiences of people who are lesbian, gay, bisexual, or transgender together under the LGBT community umbrella. However, we must recognize the unique attributes and qualities that make their experiences very different (Long & Serovich, 2003). Universal stressors to that community can be seen clearly in deprivation of civil and legal rights to validate relationships (for example, see Bepko & Johnson, 2000; Bigner, 2000). Other more ambiguous stressors are demonstrated through discrimination, bias, or even violence (Granvold & Martin, 1999).

The predominant clinical issues that reflect the influence of the oppressive culture, represent biases in gender, and influence lesbian couples' functioning are: (a) homophobia and heterosexism, (b) gender role socialization, (c) issues around identity disclosure to others, and (d) social support from the family of origin and the family of choice (Bepko & Johnson, 2000; Connolly, 2004). The role of sexism in lesbian relationships must be underscored as lesbian couples continue to be accorded only second-class status, are thwarted in attempts to legitimize their relationships, and must fight the internalization of those negative and sometimes hostile overt and covert messages (Krestan & Bepko, 1980).

Homophobia and Heterosexism

Homophobia, a "fear of" or hatred against those who are gay or lesbian, and *heterosexism*, defined by Oswald (2003) as a dynamic that elevates heterosexuality while gay, lesbian, and bisexual identities remain hidden or devalued, are insidious processes in our culture that dramatically affect lesbian couples externally and in their own internalization of these processes (Brown, 1995). By conceptualizing the human experience in strictly heterosexual terms, the lesbian, gay, and bisexual experience is consequently ignored, invalidated, and derogated (Long, 1996). A *heteronormative* stance systemically privileges the heterosexual couple and considers them the social and sexual ideal (Fields, 2001).

Brown (1995) pointed to the significance of cultural oppression. Homophobia, heterosexism, and the internalization of both of these processes affect all couples, and Brown considers them interlocking forms of oppression that can stymie lesbian couples' growth. Feelings of chronic unrest and disequilibrium can result from adapting to a hostile environment (Mallon, 1999). Additional areas of diversity, such as ethnicity and age, can lead to multiple oppressions (Reynolds & Pope, 1991).

Internalized homophobia can contribute to self-hatred and guilt and also result in pessimistic attitudes about the possibility of longevity in a same-sex relationship (Ossana, 2000). It can also wreak havoc on couple functioning, delay the coming-out process (Cabaj & Klinger, 1996), thwart identity formation, and complicate identity management (Reynolds & Hanjorgiris, 2000).

Because of the legislation and institutionalization of homophobia (Ossana, 2000; Simons, 1991), lesbian couples remain at risk for losing custody of children and being excluded from important medical decisions regarding the partner (Ossana, 2000). Major life transitions, like formalizing or dissolving relationships, must be managed in the absence of full legal or social recognition (Granvold & Martin, 1999). From an internal and interpersonal stance, these issues can challenge the very fabric of the relationship as it infiltrates the partners' private images of each other (Slater, 1995).

Heterosexism can create situations where the couple has a double bind rather than a choice: "If you are real, you may lose your family. If you hide, you may lose yourself" (Oswald, 2003, p. 128). Heterosexist norms often exclude lesbian couples from socially sanctioned rituals (Ossana, 2000) and create an atmosphere where one must accommodate and compromise the well-being of self and relationship to preserve family relations (Oswald, 2003).

In Connolly (2005), Julie, who had been coupled with Ingrid for more than 15 years, spoke about adversity and how much determination it took to have a successful relationship. She related how the societal challenges created "emotional baggage" that made her feel so "persecuted and fearful" that it became "emotionally crippling." "It's real hard to remain healthy," and she and Ingrid "devised the most incredible mental and emotional gymnastics to deal with that" on a daily basis. Martha and Nelda, together for a little over 10 years, reflected how "*dangerous* and how *tenuous*" it is to be a lesbian couple in today's world, where laws have existed prohibiting sexual intimacy between same-sex partners. Martha felt that the "whole system is set up to keep [heterosexual couples] together," but with lesbian couples, "it's just the opposite. Everything is there to get you apart" (Connolly, 2005, p. 273).

Gender Role Socialization

Gender-role socialization also has a significant effect on lesbian couples (Brown, 1995; Granvold & Martin, 1999; Ossana, 2000; Scrivner & Eldridge, 1995). As Goodrich et al. (1988) highlight, gender is a social construct; it involves the assignment of particular social tasks to one sex or the other. "These assignments define what are labeled masculine or feminine and represent social beliefs about what it means to be male and female in a given society at a particular period in time" (Goodrich et al., 1988, p. 5). While couples may share many similarities with two-gendered couples in areas such as stage of life, class, and ethnicity, they are unique in terms of gender or female/lesbian oppression (Marvin & Miller, 2000). Brown (1995) contends that both partners within a female-female relationship have more similarities due to their socialization, each holding variations of the same gender-role development, which results in both benefits and deficits to the relationship (Brown, 1995).

On the one hand, a lack of gender role constraints can produce great freedom. Similarities in gender role socialization may influence the increased emotional expressiveness (Scrivner & Eldridge, 1995), flexibility, closeness, satisfaction (Green, Bettinger, & Zacks, 1996), and egalitarianism experienced by many lesbian couples (Klinger, 1996; Laird, 1993). As Elise noted, "I think the strongest thing is that we relate to each other so well as women." Gloria, partnered with Hillary for almost 20 years, spoke about the responsibility and possibility of "establishing a relationship in which the independence is equal, dependence is mutual, and the obligation is reciprocal."

Barbara made a very strong statement about fostering competency rather than dependency in her almost-15-year relationship with Alice.

> BARBARA: I have a really strong thing about relationships and division of responsibility sometimes fostering dependence. And my examples are things like when the man dies and he has never let the wife manage money and she doesn't know what the hell is going on out there, or the woman dies and the man can't figure out how to go to the grocery store. If you all both do some of these things that if the other one were to drop off the edge of the earth tomorrow, you would be able to be a competent, functioning human being.

Shared values appeared important to many of the couples. Roberta, partnered with Quincy for over 20 years, contended that shared values for female couples might be even more important than for other couple types.

> ROBERTA: We also share the same politics. I'm not sure I could ever really love somebody who was Republican (Roberta laughs). But that–that goes back to the assumptions and the worldview (back channel by Quincy, "yeah"). We–we had a friend once who was a pretty staunch Democrat, and she got involved with a Republican and we–we just knew it wouldn't last. They just saw the world too differently. And maybe that's more important among women than among husbands and wives where people might be able to carve out their own bailiwicks. You know, "that's a guy thing." [And] since we can't do that, it's really important to have shared values.

On the other hand, Patterson and Schwartz (1994) reflect that although freedom exists, lesbian couples often lack a vision of what a lesbian couple looks like. "[C]ouples have the problem of how to telegraph to others the shape and seriousness of their commitment. They must invent some 'marital' rules, borrow others, and pick some to avoid" (Patterson & Schwartz, 1994, p. 4). Conflict can ensue as the couple deals with a multitude of issues that are taken for granted by those afforded legal status. Such often taken-for-granted things as divisions of labor, agreements on finances, whose employment or career takes priority, and recreational activities become additive and complicated factors to consider in a lesbian relationship (Swartz, 1989).

Hillary noted the early relationship "pull and tug" that was not "consciously negotiated" but rather done out of "wanting to please." She and Gloria both "were very much raised to *please* other people. And so asserting what *you* like was real hard to do. . . . And so it was very hard to learn our voice."

The participants grew up in the midst of heterosexism and saw gender role distinctions based on being male or female. Laird refers to the common cultural story, the "butch-femme narrative" (Laird, 2000a, p. 459; Laird, 2000b, p. 66), which was drawn from the larger social discourse. As a result, the word "role" often resulted in a strong reaction from participants, based on previous eras when lesbian couples "felt like they *had* to get into some kind of role . . . that one had to assume some of the male role, and one had to assume the female role."

Hillary and Gloria used a sense of humor, overt communication, and pushed gender and societal expectations to the forefront by creating "a joke" about who gets to be in "control" or "wear the lesbian tool belt."

> GLORIA: [P]eople are always sort of trying to figure out which role: "Now, does Hillary play the man, or do you?" And so we are trying to figure out those kinds of roles, and I don't know why, but for both of us the vision is that of course the one who would be playing the man would be in control. So, Hillary gets to be the man when we are driving because she likes to drive. I get to be the woman because I love to cook. So I cook. But then we go to bed and I get to be the man because I am the initiator. But then if we went out in the garden, Hillary would get to be the man because she knows what she is doing out there and has to give directions. And if we were working on woodwork or doing anything like that, it would have to be Hillary, so she gets the lesbian tool belt.

Identity Disclosure

Coming out can be a "watershed event" for anyone (Bepko & Johnson, 2000, p. 411). Yet disclosing one's affectional orientation is more than an individual decision; it also involves synchronizing and mobilizing resources for the couple's identity (Patterson, Ciabattari, & Schwartz, 1999). Often partners are at very different stages in the "coming out" process and are moving at different time schedules

(Roth, 1985), which can contribute to relational problems (Mattison & McWhirter, 1987; McWhirter & Mattison, 1996).

Important decisions are made about the stresses of invisibility and the potential pitfalls of disclosure, and lesbian couples often experience conflicting demands; they either bear the stress of invisibility or take on the stress resulting from being identifiable to the same world (Slater, 1995). Managing a bicultural life expends a tremendous amount of psychic energy (Bradford, Ryan, & Rothblum, 1994). One can experience different identities within different relationships and contexts (Savin-Williams, 1996; Slater, 1995), which can result in feelings of vigilance against any disclosure that could damage social standing or produce prejudicial or even life-threatening results (Davison, 2001).

Elise related witnessing many friends end their relationships through the years. Elise and Fran had been together for more than 20 years. She shared her view of how "being in the closet" can negatively impact couples.

> ELISE: I think that this business of being in the closet probably breaks up more people, and I don't think they realize it . . . I think it's all these pressures that they don't even realize. It's kind of a subtle thing that happens with them, and they are thinking it is something else. They are finding another excuse as to why to break up. But I just wonder if it is really–if it's not outside pressure that they can't deal with, because they haven't told their family. They haven't told their closest friends, you know.

Some individuals and couples are afforded the opportunity and intentionality to come out. However, at other times that option of choice and timing does not exist, as they are found out or "outed" (Mallon, 1999). Gloria related being "outed" at work and she and Hillary spoke of the process as being "painful" yet moving them to another "level" in their relationship.

> GLORIA: [Being outed] actually moved us to another level (back channel by Hillary, "I think so"), because it was no longer so much of an issue to keep things COMPLETELY closeted at work . . .

> HILLARY: It was like all of a sudden we knew that everybody knew . . . and so I didn't have to worry that somebody was going to say something or something was going to happen, because it had already happened. . . . And so, you know, it wasn't ever men-

tioned. It just never came up like that again . . . [We] didn't have the fear (back channel by Gloria, "right") of something coming down.

Family of Origin and Creating Family

The term *family* in the gay community is a powerful renaming and reconstituting of a traditional arrangement that historically has been difficult, at best, and abusive, at worst, for gays, lesbians, bisexuals, and transgendered persons as well as for women and children. (Halstead, 2003, p. 40)

One is typically raised in a heterosexual environment that maintains the unexamined expectations that children will not only be heterosexual (Brown, 1988; Savin-Williams, 1996) but also will marry a different-sex person and begin a traditional family (Matthews & Lease, 2000). Lesbian couples often struggle to imagine how they fit into this context (Mallon, 1999) and feel torn between the loyalty to partner and loyalty to the family of origin (Krestan & Bepko, 1980).

The lesbian woman typically does not have the same minority identification with parents, as do most ethnic and cultural minorities (Brown, 1988; Green & Mitchell, 2002). As a result, they are not able to view how parents handle issues such as prejudice and discrimination or pride in traditions (Green & Mitchell, 2002). In addition to the lack of preparation against impending discrimination, lesbian identity disclosure can be met with family hostility (Mallon, 1999). Instead of recognizing and moving away from the cultural oppression, parents and family sometimes become the main oppressor (Green, 2002; Green & Mitchell, 2002), with the family environment becoming like "living with the enemy" (Green, 2002, p. 277; Green & Mitchell, 2002, p. 557) instead of a place of refuge.

Some of the couples struggled with issues around family of origin. It seemed more pronounced in the earlier years, and time often softened relationships and allowed for strong connections. However, at the time of the interview, some relationships had not healed. For example, Hillary's parents were no longer alive, and she spoke about the "emotional toll" it would take to pursue a relationship with her remaining family members, who did not approve of her affectional orientation.

HILLARY: It doesn't mean it doesn't hurt, but it's like one of the decisions I made is I don't want to keep banging my head against it every other week, or even once a year. And so it's sort of like "It's their loss. I'm sorry, I think I'm a pretty nice person, I think I could be a nice aunt." But if they've made that decision, there really isn't anything to gain by pushing it. And some day I may do something different, but I don't know if I will. I don't know that it's worth the emotional toll it would take to do it at this point.

For others, family provided a strong sense of support. Elise and Barbara provided an example of how a family member acted as a "defender" when others made discriminatory remarks, related how it added strength to their relationship, and questioned if couples might experience a negative effect when lacking that type of support.

ELISE: [Our families] are just really good about backing us. I have a niece that is 25 or 26 and she always calls me on the phone and says, "Somebody said something today about gays and I just *reamed* into them." You know, so we have a lot of defenders out there now that we didn't have before, which is a strong thing. And I think that again helps our relationship. . . . [M]aybe people that are breaking up don't have that.

Continued family relations can be voluntary (Green, 2000; Green & Mitchell, 2002); rejection continues to be omnipresent (Green, 2000). Although lesbian couples often lack extended family support (Granvold & Martin, 1999), family can be chosen (Granvold & Martin, 1999; Patterson et al., 1999) or created (Granvold & Martin, 1999) to replace or augment family of origin. In other words, friends often become "family."

The stressors of cultural oppression, gender role socialization, identity disclosure, and special issues surrounding family of origin and created family extend across the life span. They exist in most, if not all, contexts. These stressors can result in a relational crisis, so it remains important to understand the difference between stress and stressors and to recognize processes of resilience that lesbian couples demonstrate.

RESILIENCE

Although resilience has not been consistently operationalized in the literature (O'Leary & Ickovics, 1995), a general summary of resilience is having good outcomes even in the face of serious threats (Masten,

2001), maintaining competence and effectively adapting under pressure or extreme stress (Buckley, Thórngren, & Kleist, 1998; Fraser & Richman, 1999; Masten & Coatsworth, 1998), and recovering from traumatic experiences (Fraser & Richman, 1999; Jordan & Hartling, 2002). Cowan, Cowan, and Schulz (1996) suggest that resilience, resistance to stress, or invulnerability relate to processes that function in the presence of risk to produce results as good or better than those obtained in the absence of risk. Therapists might consider a couple "at risk" when predisposed to negative or undesirable outcomes and vulnerable when facing risk when the likelihood of negative outcomes intensifies (Cowan et al., 1996).

Resilience surfaces in the face of hardship and is about buoyancy, about being able to rebound from adversity wherein one reaches or even surpasses the level of functioning that was present before the stressor or crisis (Hawley, 2000; Hawley & DeHaan, 1996). Some consider that significant risk emerges from a continuous and chronic exposure to adverse social conditions, an exposure to a traumatic event, or a combination of the two (Masten & Coatsworth, 1998; Patterson, 2002b), which is a condition prevalent in the lesbian community.

As Patterson (2002a) notes, when facing normative or significant risk, how a couple or family responds can depend on their ability to rebound, and both risk and opportunity relate not only to their internal processes but also to the social system. The amount of community resources, public programs, community institutions, as well as societal norms and values, influence family resilience. When impacted by stressors, a family's ability to accomplish their core functions can diminish and risk can escalate.

Resilience began receiving explicit attention in the 1970s, during the paradigmatic shift in focus from deficits and the debilitating effects of risk to a more positive perspective, such as adaptation, competence, and invulnerability (O'Leary & Ickovics, 1995). It was long considered a neglected construct in family therapy (Buckley et al., 1998), as resilience literature largely focused on individual health and function (Patterson, 2002a). However, resilience is an increasingly visible concept in the family therapy field (Hawley, 2000; Hawley & DeHaan, 1996), as the profession has moved away from vulnerability/deficit models to focus instead on triumphs in the face of adversity (O'Leary, 1998; O'Leary & Ickovics, 1995). Resilience is not about pathology but rather wellness (Hawley, 2000; Hawley & DeHaan, 1996), with an emphasis on strengths and resources (Hawley, 2000). Moreover, maximizing strengths is the focus rather than undoing deeply rooted damage (Buckley et al., 1998).

Previous formations suggested that resilience was a homeostatic event, wherein a family recovered and restored their equilibrium, but more recent trends recognize the movement is beyond recovery (O'Leary & Ickovics, 1995). Many couples do not just survive or recover but instead thrive under adverse circumstances (Buckley et al., 1998; Hawley, 2000).

O'Leary and Ickovics (1995) write of the transformative process of thriving. Some families struggle for survival, and others feel grateful to recover from the stressors or adversity. They effectively mobilize resources in response to the risk or threat to self or family. However, other families thrive, garnering individual resources, social resources, and responding well developmentally. Transformation typically results from a challenge that is so profound it shakes the foundation of one's life, where the sense of purpose, meaning, and/or identity are called into question.

The processes of "courage, survival, triumph [are] testimony to the resilience of spirit, but not of spirit in isolation. Rather . . . [it is the] significance of intimate alliances in supporting resilience and causing it to thrive" (Goodrich, 2003, p. 3). Women, encouraged to value connection and define self in terms of those relationships (for example, see Jordan, Kaplan, Miller, Stiver, & Surrey, 1991), often mobilize social support during times of stress to a greater degree than men (O'Leary, 1998). Some suggest that "social relationships may be key to women's resilience" (O'Leary & Ickovics, 1995, p. 132) and to their thriving (O'Leary, 1998).

Resilience is a developmental and dynamic process rather than a static entity (Hawley & DeHaan, 1996), an ongoing and often emergent process rather than a stable trait (Patterson, 2002a). Resilience also can be conceptualized from the perspective of capacity and process, with family resiliency referring to the family's *capacity* to successfully manage life circumstances and family resilience as the *process* of responding and adapting to significant crises or adversity with competence (Patterson, 2002a). Understanding these distinctions can help clarify and direct our clinical work.

Additionally, time and development are contributing factors, so viewing resilience through both a short- and long-term lens remains important (Hawley & DeHaan, 1996). Hawley (2000) posits that resilience can be conceptualized as a pathway that a family follows over time in response to one significant stressor or a series of stressors. As such, therapists can trace the path prior to and in response to stressors, as well as an anticipated future route of reorganization, thus looking both backward and forward in their family assessment. This developmental perspective does not suggest continuous care but rather repeated care over time.

RESILIENCE IN LONG-TERM LESBIAN COUPLES

In the dissertation study on strength and resilience in long-term lesbian couples (Connolly, 1999), several key processes of resilience came to the forefront (Connolly, 2005), which I will summarize below. The couples described a capacity-based relational resiliency that helped protect the relationship from external stressors. They also shared how their couple resilience provided processes they used to rebound from adversity.

Mutuality involves "openness to influence, emotional availability, and a constantly changing pattern of responding to and affecting the other's state" (Jordan, 1991, p. 82). As the couples protected against stressors, they described a relational resiliency through such a capacity for mutuality. Processes of mutuality involved personal dedication to the relationship, innovation in creating the type of relationship they wanted and needed, and synchronization of their lesbian identity. The couples also created balance in their relationship and maintained a very interdependent relationship, which supported the relationship and protected against stressors.

Couple resilience involved those processes that contributed to a rebounding from adversity. The dyads used relational unification, what Julie referred to as an "us-against-the-world" perspective, where they presented a "united front" against challenges and they would "battle whatever comes our way together." The couples also showed great determination to overcome oppression and a positive perspective to help them move beyond the adversity experienced. External buffers helped to reduce the impact of threat or harm. For some couples it came from family support, which for many developed and grew as the relationship lengthened. Others maximized friendships and created a "family of choice." All 10 couples were highly proactive in creating legal documents to fortify their relationship.

Of particular note, these long-term couples appeared to be able to compartmentalize the oppression experienced and in the first interview of two, they focused on their own strengths in the relationship. Not focusing on the burdens can be a gift to the relationship; it can also cause undue hardship to the individual and couple and at times stall healing of societal wounds.

Lesbian couples often communicate competently and effectively (Connolly & Sicola, 2005). Yet seldom are they given the privilege to speak of their relationships to others in an open and forthright way. The second interview gave an additional opportunity to hear their voices, which came through loud and clear. However, "the couples did not address the pain of real and potential loss resulting from their sexual orientation or relationship without re-prompting. The results suggest that direct prompts about experiences with adversity and oppression in a therapeutic setting might be necessary" (Connolly, 2005, p. 277).

THERAPEUTIC IMPLICATIONS

A clinician always must evaluate each individual, her life cycle stages, cultural and ethnic factors, and which processes the partners share or on which they differ. Clinicians also must assess other clinical issues that come to the fore, such as substance abuse, concerns about children, and financial problems (Cabaj & Klinger, 1996). However, special considerations exist when working with clients who manage a stigmatized identity (Dworkin, 2000).

Perez, DeBord, and Bieschke (2000) point to the need for a sharp understanding of the issues of this population and their pertinence to their clients' culture and worldview. Knowledge about the cultural history from which issues are born and awareness of the current trends in ethics, research, and practice remain critical processes. Moreover, therapists must stay acutely aware of the personal biases and assumptions that can encumber effective and ethical therapy or research.

Therapists must assess the extent to which the presenting issues are related to a lesbian identity (Scrivner & Eldridge, 1995). When working with lesbian couples, we must balance our understanding and recognition of those issues that are fundamental processes to all couples, as well as those issues that are particularly unique to lesbian couples (Basham, 1999). Striking a therapeutic balance among the affectional (Scrivner & Eldridge, 1995), affiliative (Sanders & Kroll, 2000), and sexual components of a same-sex relationship (Butler & Clarke, 1991) strengthens the clinical work. These processes provide a structure to assess specific areas unique to lesbian couples.

One must continually monitor values and norms that might have been formed by the dominant group so as not to covertly or overtly deemphasize, misconstrue, or completely overlook the strengths of women (Jordan & Hartling, 2002), lesbian women, and lesbian couples. We must be mindful of our use of gender-free language and be steadfast in educating self and clients about the lesbian and gay experience, considering referral when appropriate, and gaining awareness of relevant ethical issues (Scrivner & Eldridge, 1995). As Long and Pietsch (2004) summarize, therapists of same-sex couples must create affiliative clinical relationships, encourage multiple perspectives, focus on strengths, resiliency, and coping abilities, and acknowledge power issues both inside and outside of the therapy room.

Areas of Exploration

Specific areas of exploration include issues around identity and disclosure, the special role of the therapist in a lesbian couple's life, the distinct norms of the lesbian community, and reconsidering our assessment of lesbian couples. First, one must assess the individual and couple's lesbian identity development (Cabaj & Klinger, 1996). Learning how they self-identify, including a bisexual self-identification (Dworkin, 2000), and how they manage their identity (Reynolds & Hanjorgiris, 2000) provide important insights into the individual, relational, familial, and societal functioning. What is each person's earlier awareness of affiliation and identity? To what degree has societal homophobia and heterosexism impacted them (Reynolds & Hanjorgiris, 2000)? How has gender, culture, and/or disability affected the coming-out process (Dworkin, 2000)? All of these areas can influence the therapy process.

A second area to explore includes their past, present, or possibly future coming-out process. However, instead of viewing whether one discloses or not as a marker of mental health and adjustment, it simply may reflect a client's realistic assessment of real or potential consequences, and therapists must allow clients to make those choices and not assume a must-disclose attitude (Green, 2000, 2002; Green & Mitchell, 2002). In order to validate a same-sex relationship, one must understand the culture of the couple, value the process of their struggle, and recognize that the coming-out process is a "profoundly personal, political, and spiritual process of knowing self in relationship to other" (Halstead, 2003, p. 48).

Another important consideration is to recognize the special role of the therapist in the couple process. Lesbian couples manage their major life and relational transitions, including formalizing and dissolving their relationship, without the rituals and mutually recognized traditions afforded different-sex couples (Granvold & Martin, 1999). As a result, the therapist often plays the role of historian (Schiemann & Smith, 1996) and witness to the relationship (Simons, 1991). Therapists can refuel the relational viability, nullify the internalized homophobic messages, and verify and validate their family status (Slater & Mencher, 1991), which serve to support their relationships and facilitate life transitions.

Fourth, a unique process of grief can emerge and often a full-grief cycle exists for the entire family (Matthews & Lease, 2000). Few sanctions or socially acceptable processes for mourning losses associated with same-sex relationships exist (Krestan & Bepko, 1980). Couples experience the loss of "heterosexual privilege" in their family of origin (Young & Long, 1998). Homophobia can leave the client vulnerable to self-blame, shame, and helplessness, so externalizing various aspects of the presenting issue can prove helpful (Bepko & Johnson, 2000).

Finally, we must honor the distinct norms of lesbian couples. The therapist must be sensitive and aware of cultural norms when exploring and determining who should be a part of the therapeutic process. Those traditional concepts of blood- or legal-based tradition cannot be emphasized over the couple's "family of choice," and the latter often determines who should be in therapy sessions (Bepko & Johnson, 2000). According to Bepko and Johnson (2000), to work effectively with lesbian couples, one also must strive to avoid pathologizing behavior that may be normative for couples in that community. Because of different norms, lesbian couples can assign different meanings to all of life's areas including sexual exclusivity, relationships with family, extended family, family of choice, and the place of former partners in the couple's life. We also must explore the amount of connection or support the client does draw or might gain from the lesbian community (Scrivner & Eldridge, 1995). Involvement with the community appears to positively affect the well-being of lesbian women (Toder, 1992). As therapists, we must recognize that "Anywhere that lesbians congregate can become a sanctuary. . . . Lesbian women look to the lesbian community for fellowship, sisterhood, family, and kindred spirits" (Goodrich et al., 1988, p. 144).

Processes to Consider

While feminist family therapy provides a strong foundation when working with lesbian couples, therapists must remain ever-aware of blind spots and biases (Caplan, 1992). As Akamatsu, Basham, and

Olson (1996) note, a strong feminist perspective might overshadow perspectives on other oppressive contexts and create tunnel vision. We must develop the type of reflexivity that allows us to both notice and receive diverse perspectives. Unless we stand outside of and observe self, we might overestimate identification and underestimate difference. "The therapist may believe that sharing womanhood with her lesbian clients is so fundamental a similarity as to render insignificant any dissimilarity arising from the lesbian experience" (Goodrich et al., 1988, p. 159). McLeod's (1994) analysis of women's experience of feminist therapy and counseling provides an example. Some women expressed marginalization by differential experiences, including lesbian women, older women, and women of different socioeconomic backgrounds. While the therapist does not necessarily need first-hand experience, it is also important not to assume that just because the therapist is a woman, that she understands the experience of all women.

Goodrich et al. (1988) points to several other areas to monitor when working with lesbian couples: (a) failing to recognize mutually shared homophobia and heterosexist bias, (b) maintaining a hands-off policy and being reluctant to address issues that one would address when working with a heterosexual couple, (c) classifying clients by their sexual orientation rather than by their presentation in therapy, and (d) idealizing the lesbian experience and only focusing on the strengths. The authors note the importance of assessing the impact of the sociopolitical, intrapsychic, and familial processes, but they also remind us not to overlook the physiological ones (Caplan, 1992).

Additionally, therapists must review stressors and methods of coping. Slater (1995) emphasizes that many family therapists view repeated confrontation of the same stresses and use of the same coping mechanism as necessarily reflective of problems in development or flaws in coping abilities. Instead, it may result from and be a realistic estimate of the impact of those immutable cultural stressors. Lesbian couples function in an oppressive society and the couple's key difficulties may result from the sustained stress that is part of being a lesbian woman and couple in this culture. Naming these stressors can increase relational confidence and often stabilize the crisis or couple.

As has been described above, lesbian couples experience a tremendous amount of external stressors, and it will take massive social change to eliminate these stressors. However, as Slater (1995) underscores, we can help clients understand the nature and origin of those stressors. In doing so, therapists help protect couples from over-personalizing the source of their struggle and facilitate couples to develop creative responses to safeguard their relationship. Activism remains an important part of being a feminist family therapist. Lesbian and gay families are at the "intersection of the psychological with the sociological and the political. Homonegativity is a societal disorder, and the remedy is ultimately to be found in social change" (Martin, 1998, p. 287). Some argue that it is impossible to practice positive, affirmative therapy with clients without also attending to social injustices and global oppression (Carroll & Gilroy, 2002).

CONCLUSIONS

Diversity in systems is to be understood and respected (Halstead, 2003). Culture is "the design, the tapestry portraying all of the ways a particular group of people has lived throughout their history. We must view our clients' cultures with reverence and intelligence" (Halstead, 2003, p. 49). As such, therapists must continue the assessment of lesbian identity development and its intersection with other ethnic, cultural, religious, and professional identities (Scrivner & Eldridge, 1995).

Worell (2001) emphasizes the complex interplay between the internal and external processes in women's lives and the importance of feminist interventions, which are aimed toward promoting women's safety, positive life-styles, strengths, competence, and resilience. According to Worell, these interventions are planned to prevent, educate, remediate, empower, and work toward community change and are aimed at holding professionals accountable beyond the reduction of symptoms.

Despite phrases like *postfeminist era*, discrimination against women is still pervasive (Goodrich, 2003). No matter how strongly aligned a therapist is with feminist therapy, certain biases from a sexist culture and traces of that social conditioning subsist (Haddock et al., 2000). As Goodrich (2003) notes, "the effects of misogyny are small, personal, individual as well as large, sweeping, systematic" (p. 5). Slights that might seem too small to mention end up with enormous consequences, and sexist events can jeopardize both physical and mental health.

Awareness is important but it is not enough; we must examine our own lack of approbation as therapists, regardless of our sexual or affectional orientation (Schiemann & Smith, 1996). We must not simply notice the issues but instead *raise* the issues (Parker, 2003) and ask the difficult questions both of our clients (Caplan, 1992) and of ourselves. This important reconceptualization and re-languaging of lesbian couples' resilience, paramount in today's application of family therapy, creates dialogue that can result in controversy and conflict but also in healing and growth.

This article explored stressors associated with being a lesbian couple and how their processes of resilience help to form and maintain long-lasting and successful relationships. We must not only hear but speak from a nondominant perspective, which serves to open the door wider for discovering lesbian couples' stressors and resilience. If we proactively unpack societal injunctions as to what a relationship "should" look like, we then can help lesbian couples create the type of relationship that works best for them, including those variations from the norm that are part of the process of resilience and serve to protect the integrity of the couple and fortify relational success.

REFERENCES

Akamatsu, N. N., Basham, K., & Olson, M. (1996). Teaching a feminist family therapy. In K. Weingarten & M. Bograd (Eds.), *Reflections of feminist family therapy training* (pp. 21-36). New York: The Haworth Press, Inc.

Basham, K. K. (1999). Therapy with a lesbian couple: The art of balancing lenses. In J. Laird (Ed.), *Lesbians and lesbian families: Reflections on theory and practice* (pp. 143-177). New York: Columbia University Press.

Bepko, C., & Johnson, T. (2000). Gay and lesbian couples in therapy: Perspectives for the contemporary family therapist. *Journal of Marital and Family Therapy, 26*(4), 409-419.

Bigner, J. J. (2000). Gay and lesbian families. In W. C. Nichols, M. S. Pace-Nichols, D. S. Becvar, & A. Y. Napier (Eds.), *Handbook of family development and intervention* (pp. 279-298). New York: John Wiley & Sons.

Boss, P. (1988). *Family stress management.* Newbury Park, CA: Sage.

Bradford, J., Ryan, C., & Rothblum, E. D. (1994). National lesbian health care survey: Implications for mental health care. *Journal of Consulting and Clinical Psychology, 62*(2), 228-242.

Brown, L. S. (1988). Lesbians, gay men, and their families: Common clinical issues. *Journal of Gay & Lesbian Psychotherapy, 1*(1), 65-77.

Brown, L. S. (1991). Commentary on the special issue of The Counseling Psychologist: Counseling with lesbians and gay men. *Counseling Psychologist, 19*(2), 235-238.

Brown, L. S. (1995). Therapy with same-sex couples: An introduction. In N. S. Jacobson & A. S. Gurman (Eds.), *Clinical handbook of couple therapy* (pp. 274-291). New York: Guilford Press.

Buckley, M. R., Thorngren, J. M., & Kleist, D. M. (1998). Family resiliency: A neglected family construct. *The Family Journal: Counseling and Therapy for Couples and Families, 5*(3), 241-246.

Butler, M., & Clarke, J. (1991). Couple therapy with homosexual men. In D. Hooper & W. Dryden (Eds.), *Couple therapy: A handbook* (pp. 196-206). Philadelphia: Open University Press.

Cabaj, R. P., & Klinger, R. L. (1996). Psychotherapeutic interventions with lesbian and gay couples. In R. P. Cabaj & T. S. Stein (Eds.), *Textbook of homosexuality and mental health* (pp. 485-501). Washington, DC: American Psychiatric Press.

Caplan, P. J. (1992). Driving us crazy: How oppression damages women's mental health and what we can do about it. *Women & Therapy, 12*(3), 5-28.

Carroll, L., & Gilroy, P. J. (2002). Transgender issues in counselor preparation. *Counselor Education & Supervision, 41*(3), 233-242.

Connolly, C. M. (1999). Lesbian couples: A qualitative study of strengths and resilient factors in long-term relationships. *Dissertation Abstracts International, 59*(7-A), 2358. (UMI No. 9838850)

Connolly, C. M. (2004). Clinical issues with same-sex couples: A review of the literature. In J. Wetchler & J. Bigner (Eds.), *Relationship therapy with same-sex couples* (pp. 3-12). New York: The Haworth Press, Inc.

Connolly, C. M. (2005). A qualitative exploration of resilience in long-term lesbian couples. *The Family Journal: Counseling and Therapy for Couples and Families, 13*(3), 266-280.

Connolly, C. M., & Sicola, M. K. (2005). Listening to lesbian couples: Communication competence in long-term relationships. *Journal of GLBT Family Studies: Innovations in Theory, Research, and Practice, 1*(2), 143-168.

Cowan, P. A., Cowan, C. P., & Schulz, M. S. (1996). Thinking about risk and resilience in families. In E. M. Hetherington & E. A. Blechman (Eds.), *Stress, coping, and resiliency in children and families* (pp. 1-38). Hillsdale, NJ: Lawrence Erlbaum Associates, Inc.

Davison, G. C. (2001). Conceptual and ethical issues in therapy for the psychological problems of gay men, lesbians, and bisexuals. *Journal of Clinical Psychology, 57*(5), 695-704.

Dworkin, S. (2000). Individual therapy with lesbian, gay, and bisexual clients. In R. M. Perez, K. A. DeBord, & K. J. Bieschke (Eds.), *Handbook of counseling and psychotherapy with lesbian, gay, and bisexual clients* (pp. 157-181). Washington, DC: American Psychological Association.

Fields, J. (2001). Normal queers: Straight parents respond to their children's "coming out." *Symbolic Interaction, 24*(2), 165-187.

Fraser, M. W., & Richman, J. M. (1999). Risk, protection, and resilience: Toward a conceptual framework for social work practice [Electronic version]. *Social Work Research, 23*(3), 318-342.

Goldner, V. (1989). Generation and gender: Normative and covert hierarchies. In M. McGoldrick & C. M. Anderson (Eds.), *Women in families: A framework for family therapy* (pp. 42-60). New York: W. W. Norton.

Goodrich, T. J. (2003). A feminist family therapist's work is never done. In L. B. Silverstein & T. J. Goodrich (Eds.), *Feminist family therapy: Empowerment in social context* (pp. 3-15).Washington, DC: American Psychological Association.

Goodrich, T. J., Rampage, C., Ellman, B., & Halstead, K. (1988). *Feminist family therapy: A casebook*. New York: W. W. Norton.

Granvold, D. K., & Martin, J. I. (1999). Family therapy with gay and lesbian clients. In C. Franklin & C. Jordan (Eds.), *Family practice: Brief systems methods for social work* (pp. 299-320). Pacific Grove, CA: Brooks/Cole.

Green, R. J. (2000). "Lesbians, gay men, and their parents": A critique of LaSala and the prevailing clinical "wisdom." *Family Process, 39*(2), 257-266.

Green, R. J. (2002). Coming out to family . . . in context. In E. Davis-Russell (Ed.), *The California School of Professional Psychology handbook of multicultural education, research, intervention, and training* (pp. 277-284). San Francisco: Jossey-Bass.

Green, R. J., Bettinger, M., & Zacks, E. (1996). Are lesbian couples fused and gay male couples disengaged? Questioning gender straightjackets. In J. Laird & R.-J. Green (Eds.), *Lesbians and gays in couples and families: A handbook for therapists.* San Francisco: Jossey-Bass.

Green, R. J., & Mitchell, V. (2002). Gay and lesbian couples in therapy: Homophobia, relational ambiguity, and social support. In A. S. Gurman & N. S. Jacobson (Eds.), *Clinical handbook of couple therapy* (pp. 536-568). New York: Guilford Press.

Greene, B. (1994). Lesbian women of color: Triple jeopardy. In L. Comas-Díaz & B. Greene (Eds.), *Women of color: Integrating ethnic and gender identities in psychotherapy* (pp. 389-427). New York: Guilford.

Haddock, S. A., Zimmerman, T. S., & MacPhee, D. (2000). The power equity guide: Attending to gender in family therapy. *Journal of Marital and Family Therapy, 26*(2), 153-170.

Halstead, K. (2003). Over the rainbow: The lesbian family. In L. B. Silverstein & J. T. Goodrich (Eds.), *Feminist family therapy: Empowerment in social context* (pp. 39-50). Washington, DC: American Psychological Association.

Hawley, D. R. (2000). Clinical implications of family resilience. *The American Journal of Family Therapy, 28,* 101-116.

Hawley, D. R., & DeHaan, L. (1996). Toward a definition of family resilience: Integrating life-span and family perspectives. *Family Process, 35*(3), 283-298.

Jordan, J. V. (1991). The meaning of mutuality. In J. V. Jordan, A. G. Kaplan, J. B. Miller, I. P. Stiver, & J. L. Surrey (Eds.), *Women's growth in connection: Writings from the Stone Center* (pp. 81-96). New York: Guilford Press.

Jordan, J. V., & Hartling, L. M. (2002). New developments in Relational-Cultural Theory. In M. Ballou & L. S. Brown (Eds.), *Rethinking mental health and disorder: Feminist perspectives* (pp. 48-70). New York, NY: Guilford Press.

Jordan, J. V., Kaplan, A. G., Miller, J. B., Stiver, I. P., & Surrey, J. L. (1991). *Women's growth in connection: Writings from the Stone Center.* New York: Guilford Press.

Klinger, R. L. (1996). Lesbian couples. In R. P. Cabaj & T. S. Stein (Eds.), *Textbook of homosexuality and mental health* (pp. 339-352). Washington, DC: American Psychiatric Press.

Krestan, J. A., & Bepko, C. S. (1980). The problem of fusion in the lesbian relationship. *Family Process, 19,* 277-289.

Laird, J. (1993). Lesbian and gay families. In F. Walsh (Ed.), *Normal family processes* (2nd ed., pp. 282-328). New York: Guilford Press.

Laird, J. (2000a). Gender in lesbian relationships: Cultural, feminist, and constructionist reflections. *Journal of Marital and Family Therapy, 26*(4), 455-467.

Laird, J. (2000b). Gender and sexuality in lesbian relationships: Feminist and constructionist perspectives. In J. Laird (Ed.), *Lesbians and lesbian families: Reflections on theory and practice* (pp. 47-89). New York: Columbia University Press.

Long, J. K. (1996). Working with lesbians, gays, and bisexuals: Addressing heterosexism in supervision. *Family Process, 35*(3), 377-388.

Long, J. K., & Pietsch, U. K. (2004). How do therapists of same-sex couples "do it"? In S. Greene & D. Flemons (Eds.), *Quickies: Brief approaches to sex therapy* (pp. 171-188). New York: Norton.

Long, J. K., & Serovich, J. M. (2003). Incorporating sexual orientation into MFT training programs: Infusion and inclusion. *Journal of Marital and Family Therapy, 29*(1), 59-68.

Mallon, G. P. (1999). Gay and lesbian adolescents and their families. *Journal of Gay & Lesbian Social Services, 10*(2), 69-88.

Martin, A. (1998). Clinical issues in psychotherapy with lesbian-, gay-, and bisexual-parented families. In C. Patterson & A. R. D'Augelli (Eds.), *Lesbian, gay, and bisexual identities in families: Psychological perspectives* (pp. 270-291). New York: Oxford.

Marvin, C., & Miller, D. (2000). Lesbian couples entering the 21st century. In P. Papp (Ed.), *Couples on the fault line* (pp. 257-283). New York: Guilford.

Masten, A. S. (2001). Ordinary magic: Resilience processes in development. *American Psychologist, 56*(3), 227-238.

Masten, A. S., & Coatsworth, J. D. (1998). The development of competence in favorable and unfavorable environments: Lessons from research on successful children. *American Psychologist, 53*(2), 205-220.

Mathews, B., & Paradise, L. V. (1988). Toward methodological diversity: Qualitative research approaches. *Journal of Mental Health Counseling, 10*(4), 225-234.

Matthews, C. R., & Lease, S. H. (2000). Focus on lesbian, gay, and bisexual families. In R. M. Perez, K. A. DeBord, & K. J. Bieschke (Eds.), *Handbook of counseling and psychotherapy with lesbian, gay, and bisexual clients* (pp. 249-273). Washington, DC: American Psychological Association.

Mattison, A. M., & McWhirter, D. P. (1987). Stage discrepancy in male couples. *Journal of Homosexuality, 14*, 89-99.

May, K. M. (2001). Feminist family therapy defined. In K. M. May (Ed.), *Feminist family therapy* (pp. 3-14). Alexandria, VA: American Counseling Association.

McLeod, E. (1994). *Women's experience of feminist therapy and counseling.* Buckingham, England: Open University Press.

McWhirter, D. P., & Mattison, A. M. (1996). Male couples. In R. P. Cabaj & T. S. Stein (Eds.), *Textbook of homosexuality and mental health* (pp. 319-337). Washington, DC: American Psychiatric Press.

Morgan, K. S., & Brown, L. S. (1991). Lesbian career development, work behavior, and vocational counseling. *Counseling Psychologist, 19*(2), 273-291.

O'Leary, V. E. (1998). Strength in the face of adversity: Individual and social striving. *Journal of Social Issues, 54*(2), 425-446.

O'Leary, V. E., & Ickovics, J. R. (1995). Resilience and thriving in response to challenge: An opportunity for a paradigm shift in women's health. *Women's Health: Research on Gender, Behavior, and Policy, 1*(2) 121-142.

Ossana, S. M. (2000). Relationship and couples counseling. In R. M. Perez, K. A. DeBord, & K. J. Bieschke (Eds.), *Handbook of counseling and psychotherapy with lesbian, gay, and bisexual clients* (pp. 275-302). Washington, DC: American Psychological Association.

Oswald, R. F. (2003). A member of the wedding? Heterosexism and family ritual. *Journal of Lesbian Studies, 7*(2), 107-131.

Parker, L. (2003). Bringing power from the margins to the center. In L. B. Silverstein & J. T. Goodrich (Eds.), *Feminist family therapy: Empowerment in social context* (pp. 225-238). Washington, DC: American Psychological Association.

Patterson, D. G., Ciabattari, T., & Schwartz, P. (1999). The constraints of innovation: Commitment and stability among same-sex couples. In J. M. Adams & W. H. Jones (Eds.), *Handbook of interpersonal commitment and relationship stability*. New York: Kluwer Academic/Plenum Publishers.

Patterson, D. G., & Schwartz, P. (1994). The social construction of conflict in intimate same-sex couples. In D. D. Cahn (Ed.), *Conflict in personal relationships* (pp. 3-26). Hillsdale, NJ: Erlbaum.

Patterson, J. M. (2002a). Integrating family resilience and family stress theory [Electronic version]. *Journal of Marriage & Family, 64*(2), 349-360.

Patterson, J. M. (2002b). Understanding family resilience [Electronic version]. *Journal of Clinical Psychology, 58*(3), 233-246.

Perez, R. M., DeBord, K. A., & Bieschke, K. J. (2000). Introduction: The challenge of awareness, knowledge, and action. In R. M. Perez, K. A. DeBord, & K. J. Bieschke (Eds.), *Handbook of counseling and psychotherapy with lesbian, gay, and bisexual clients* (pp. 3-8). Washington, DC: American Psychological Association.

Rampage, C. (1995). Gendered aspects of marital therapy. In N. S. Jacobson & A. S. Gurman (Eds.), *Clinical handbook of couple therapy* (pp. 261-273). New York: Guilford Press.

Rampage, C. (1996). On being a feminist trainer in an independent institute. In K. Weingarten & M. Bograd (Eds.), *Reflections of feminist family therapy training* (pp. 7-19). New York: The Haworth Press, Inc.

Rampage, C. (1998). Feminist couple therapy. In F. M. Dattilio (Ed.), *Case studies in couple and family therapy: Systemic and cognitive perspectives* (pp. 353-370). New York: Guilford Press.

Reynolds, A. L., & Hanjorgiris, W. F. (2000). Coming out: Lesbian, gay, and bisexual identity development. In R. M. Perez, K. A. DeBord, & K. J. Bieschke (Eds.), *Handbook of counseling and psychotherapy with lesbian, gay, and bisexual clients* (pp. 35-55). Washington, DC: American Psychological Association.

Reynolds, A. L., & Pope, R. L. (1991). The complexities of diversity: Exploring multiple oppressions. *Journal of Counseling & Development, 70*(10), 174-180.

Roth, S. (1985). Psychotherapy with lesbian couples: Individual issues, female socialization, and the social context. *Journal of Marital and Family Therapy 11*(3), 273-286.

Rothberg, B. R., & Ubell, V. (1987). Feminist and systems theory: Its impact on lesbian and heterosexual couples. In C. M. Brody (Ed.), *Women's therapy groups: Paradigms of feminist treatment* (pp. 132-144). New York: Spring Publishing.

Sanders, G. L., & Kroll, I. T. (2000). Generating stories of resilience: Helping gay and lesbian youth and their families. *Journal of Marital and Family Therapy, 26*(4), 433-442.

Savin-Williams, R. C. (1996). Self-labeling and disclosure among gay, lesbian, and bisexual youths. In J. Laird & R.-J. Green (Eds.), *Lesbians and gays in couples and families: A handbook for therapists* (pp. 153-182). San Francisco: Jossey-Bass.

Schiemann, J., & Smith, W. L. (1996). The homosexual couple. In H. Kessler & I. D. Yalom (Eds.), *Treating couples.* San Francisco: Jossey-Bass.

Scrivner, R., & Eldridge, N. S. (1995). Lesbian and gay family psychology. In R. H. Mikesell, D. Lusterman, & S. H. McDaniel (Eds.), *Integrating family therapy: Handbook of family psychology and systems theory* (pp. 327-344). Washington, DC: American Psychological Association.

Seem, S. R. (2001). Feminist family therapy: For heterosexual couples only? In K. M. May (Ed.), *Feminist family therapy* (pp. 29-51). Alexandria, VA: American Counseling Association.

Simons, S. (1991). Couple therapy with lesbians. In D. Hooper & W. Dryden (Eds.), *Couple therapy: A handbook* (pp. 207-216). Bristol, PA: Open University Press.

Slater, S. (1995). *The lesbian family life cycle.* New York: Free Press.

Slater, S., & Mencher, J. (1991). The lesbian family life cycle: A contextual approach. *American Journal of Orthopsychiatry, 61*(3), 372-382.

Swartz, V. J. (1989). Relational therapy with lesbian couples. In G. R. Weeks (Ed.), *Treating couples: The intersystem model of the Marriage Council of Philadelphia* (pp. 236-257). New York: Brunner/Mazel.

Toder, N. (1992). Lesbian couples in particular. In B. Berzon (Ed.), *Positively gay: New approaches to gay and lesbian life* (pp. 50-63). Berkeley, CA: Celestial Arts.

Worell, J. (2001). Feminist interventions: Accountability beyond symptom reduction. *Psychology of Women Quarterly, 25*(4), 335-343.

Young, M. E., & Long, L. L. (1998). *Counseling and therapy for couples.* Pacific Grove: Brooks/Cole.

doi:10.1300/J086v18n01_06

Reflection:
"Girls Can't Marry Other Girls"

Lisa Giddings

Out of the blue the other day, on the way to breakfast, she said mat-ter-of-factly: "Girls can't marry other girls." We looked at each other and both felt that same punched-in-the-gut feeling.

"JackKelly said so."

My mind whirled. I immediately got defensive. What does being able to marry have to do with commitment?

How can you have a discussion around the politics of the Defense of Marriage Act with a preschooler, however precocious? What kind of Sex-and-the-City conversations is she having with this kid? The other day she said "JackKelly doesn't like me *that* way.". . . I wanted to ask *"what* way?" but decided that I didn't want to know the answer. I imag-ine them debating the constraints of monogamy and commitment over milk and Goldfish crackers at snack time. I envision his easy let-down: "Maggie, it's not you, it's me . . . "

Furthermore, what kind of conversations is JackKelly having with his *parents*?

"That's just not true, Maggie" I implored. "Your mom and I are mar-ried!"

A lie.

We daydreamed about running off to Banff, or Boston, or San Fran-cisco. We'd whisk off with a couple of witnesses and get a paper to offer

[Haworth co-indexing entry note]: "Reflection: 'Girls Can't Marry Other Girls'." Giddings, Lisa. Co-published simultaneously in *Journal of Feminist Family Therapy* (The Haworth Press, Inc.) Vol. 18, No. 1/2, 2006, pp. 163-166; and: *Lesbian Families' Challenges and Means of Resiliency: Implications for Feminist Family Therapy* (ed: Anne M. Prouty Lyness) The Haworth Press, Inc., 2006, pp. 163-166. Single or multiple copies of this article are available for a fee from The Haworth Document Delivery Service [1-800-HAWORTH, 9:00 a.m. - 5:00 p.m. (EST). E-mail address: docdelivery@haworthpress.com].

Available online at http://jfft.haworthpress.com
doi:10.1300/J086v18n01_07

her some kind of legal and, therefore, legitimate proof of our commitment to each other when–in some time *way* in the future when she's 21 or something–we hoped to put off this line of dialogue. Going to Banff would be like eloping but we're too old for our parents to care. Plus, it wouldn't be as much fun as Vegas (I don't think there's been an Elvis sighting on Lake Louise). Anyway, it wouldn't legally even count upon our return to Minnesota. That's the debate we're having among ourselves. Maybe we are simply justifying an expensive vacation.

I resorted to Maggie's rushed, illogical style of argument: "But Mom let me have candy before bed *last* night!" If I pile on the evidence thinking maybe she'll be convinced: "But Maggie, Barb and Lynn across the street are married. And Chris and Annie are married. And Tommy and Joey . . ."

I doth protest too much.

At breakfast through the lethargic language of spelling we debated our options. "Should we C-O-N-F-R-O-N-T his P-A-R-E-N-T-S and ask them why they told him that girls can't M-A-R-R-Y other G-I-R-L-S?" It's like speaking in code in front of an NSA agent, though, because she is prematurely learning to spell, or at least learning to piece together some meaning from the pronounced words among the spelled-out ones in the way that one can step back and tell what the puzzle will look like long before it is finished. "WHOSE PARENTS???" She asked. Soon we'll be learning Bulgarian or some other obscure Slavic language just to be able to discuss sensitive matters in her presence as I suspect Pig Latin is already neatly under her belt.

It all felt like a betrayal to me. I haven't felt ashamed of being gay since I was 15 and caught fumbling with my first girlfriend in the basement of our small-town-Nebraska home. That constant fear of footsteps on the stairs. That panicked jump to the other side of the couch followed by that self-conscious absorption of whatever documentary the television had fallen to by happenstance prior to the *tête-a-tête*. Coming out of the closet was a liberating experience, but here I was right back inside it; our daughter, one of those footsteps on the stairs! A republican in three-year-old's clothing defending the true state of marriage as between a man and a woman. In her case, between Barbie and Ken at least. (Despite our best attempts, keeping the disproportionately sized and oppressive female figures out of the house was impossible, and her devotion to the dolls has, over time, become tolerable. She has, after all, her own will).

I moved to Minneapolis from Washington D.C. and was struck by the difference in commitment between the two towns. No one is committed in Washington D.C. Everything is on the political four-year-cycle. Relationships, restaurants, neighborhoods, jobs, everything. I once heard a story on *This American Life* about a corner in the *Adams Morgan* neighborhood, which served as a revolving door for various shops and restaurants. During my six year graduate school stint in the close to, but cheaper and therefore more dangerous than, neighborhood misnamed *Mount Pleasant* with its urine fragrance, I witnessed at least seven different businesses on that corner.

My one serious relationship during that period of my life was no exception. I remember one conversation we had after we had been living together for over a year in which she emphatically asked me not to put my stuff on her dresser as she didn't want it to mingle with her's. It would, after all, be much more difficult to split up when she would leave.

I met my long-time partner in Minneapolis, Minnesota. At the time of our meeting, literally all of her friends had been in 10-year committed relationships whereas none of my friends were even dating anyone on a steady basis. Okay, one couple was approaching the two-year mark, but even they were on the rocks. And it wasn't just a difference in couples and relationships. People in the Twin Cities seemed committed to everything: their city, their community, their local mom-and-pop hardware store, and their gardens (Minneapolosians crowd into *Bachman's,* the local garden chain and drop hundreds-even thousands–of dollars each May in preparation for the shortened growing season). Furthermore, everyone in the Twin Cities is *from* the Twin Cities. The area is notoriously hard on newcomers who can't break into the social circles consisting of extended families and deeply-rooted neighbors.

When I landed a job in the Twin Cities area, I welcomed what I perceived as a culture of commitment and practically fulfilled a lesbian one-liner by U-Hauling into her life on the second date. She is the epitome of Minnesota commitment, having lived no more than one short hour away from her parents (during college) and even then returning on weekends for laundering and reassurance, ultimately moving back into their home during law school. Whenever we attempt to leave the region for even the shortest of visits, some barrier blocks our attempts: a forgotten cell-phone, a family emergency, or a fender-bender. We've even considered moving across town to be within walking distance to Maggie's kindergarten but we're too committed to our neighbors to leave them.

So what difference does a piece of paper make when we are at least as committed to each other as our heterosexually-oriented-legally-married counterparts? Does not a commitment by any other name smell as sweet? I thought it made no difference. At least until breakfast that day. I had no retort, after all, to JackKelly. Girls, in fact, cannot get married to other girls.

On the way home from Maggie's preschool the other day, I tiptoed around the random patches of ice on the sidewalk with Maggie on my shoulders, heavy from a day's worth of experience. I bring up only innocuous things. "Did you like the PB and J in your lunch?" Of course, the topic of marriage is the least of our worries. Wait until she hears our version of the birds and the bees. I can just imagine it: "Mom, where do babies come from?" "Well Maggie, there was this poor med student out in Berkeley. . ." As we approached the street she said, matter-of-factly, "Dinosaurs can't get married." This gave me some perspective. At least, for now, she's on to a new dilemma; the fact that her two moms can't get married according to JackKelly doesn't worry her for long. Maybe we can protect her from such concerns until she's old enough to form her own opinion. Maybe not.

Index

Numbers followed by *f* denote references to figures.

BOOK ORDER FORM!

Order a copy of this book with this form or online at:
http://www.HaworthPress.com/store/product.asp?sku= 5937

Lesbian Families' Challenges and Means of Resiliency
Implications for Feminist Family Therapy

_____ in softbound at $25.00 ISBN-13: 978-0-7890-3428-1 / ISBN-10: 0-7890-3428-X.
_____ in hardbound at $45.00 ISBN-13: 978-0-7890-3427-4 / ISBN-10: 0-7890-3427-1.

COST OF BOOKS _____

POSTAGE & HANDLING _____
US: $4.00 for first book & $1.50
for each additional book
Outside US: $5.00 for first book
& $2.00 for each additional book.

SUBTOTAL _____

In Canada: add 6% GST. _____

STATE TAX _____
CA, IL, IN, MN, NJ, NY, OH, PA & SD residents
please add appropriate local sales tax.

FINAL TOTAL _____
If paying in Canadian funds, convert
using the current exchange rate,
UNESCO coupons welcome.

❑ **BILL ME LATER:**
Bill-me option is good on US/Canada/
Mexico orders only; not good to jobbers,
wholesalers, or subscription agencies.

❑ **Signature** _____

❑ **Payment Enclosed: $**_____

❑ **PLEASE CHARGE TO MY CREDIT CARD:**

❑ Visa ❑ MasterCard ❑ AmEx ❑ Discover
❑ Diner's Club ❑ Eurocard ❑ JCB

Account #_____

Exp Date_____

Signature_____
(Prices in US dollars and subject to change without notice.)

PLEASE PRINT ALL INFORMATION OR ATTACH YOUR BUSINESS CARD

Name

Address

City   State/Province   Zip/Postal Code

Country

Tel   Fax

E-Mail

May we use your e-mail address for confirmations and other types of information? ❑ Yes ❑ No We appreciate receiving
your e-mail address. Haworth would like to e-mail special discount offers to you, as a preferred customer.
We will never share, rent, or exchange your e-mail address. We regard such actions as an invasion of your privacy.

Order from your **local bookstore** or directly from
The Haworth Press, Inc. 10 Alice Street, Binghamton, New York 13904-1580 • USA
Call our toll-free number (1-800-429-6784) / Outside US/Canada: (607) 722-5857
Fax: 1-800-895-0582 / Outside US/Canada: (607) 771-0012
E-mail your order to us: orders@HaworthPress.com

For orders outside US and Canada, you may wish to order through your local
sales representative, distributor, or bookseller.
For information, see http://HaworthPress.com/distributors

(Discounts are available for individual orders in US and Canada only, not booksellers/distributors.)

Please photocopy this form for your personal use.
www.HaworthPress.com

BOF06